AF593500

I would like to give you a message. Please do your best to tell the world what is happening to us, so that other children don't have to pass through this violence.

A 15-year-old girl who escaped from the Lord's Resistance Army in Uganda

child soldiers

EDITED BY LEORA KAHN
INTRODUCTION BY LUIS MORENO-OCAMPO

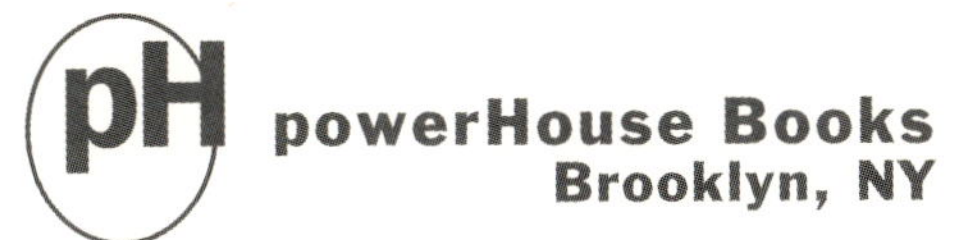
powerHouse Books
Brooklyn, NY

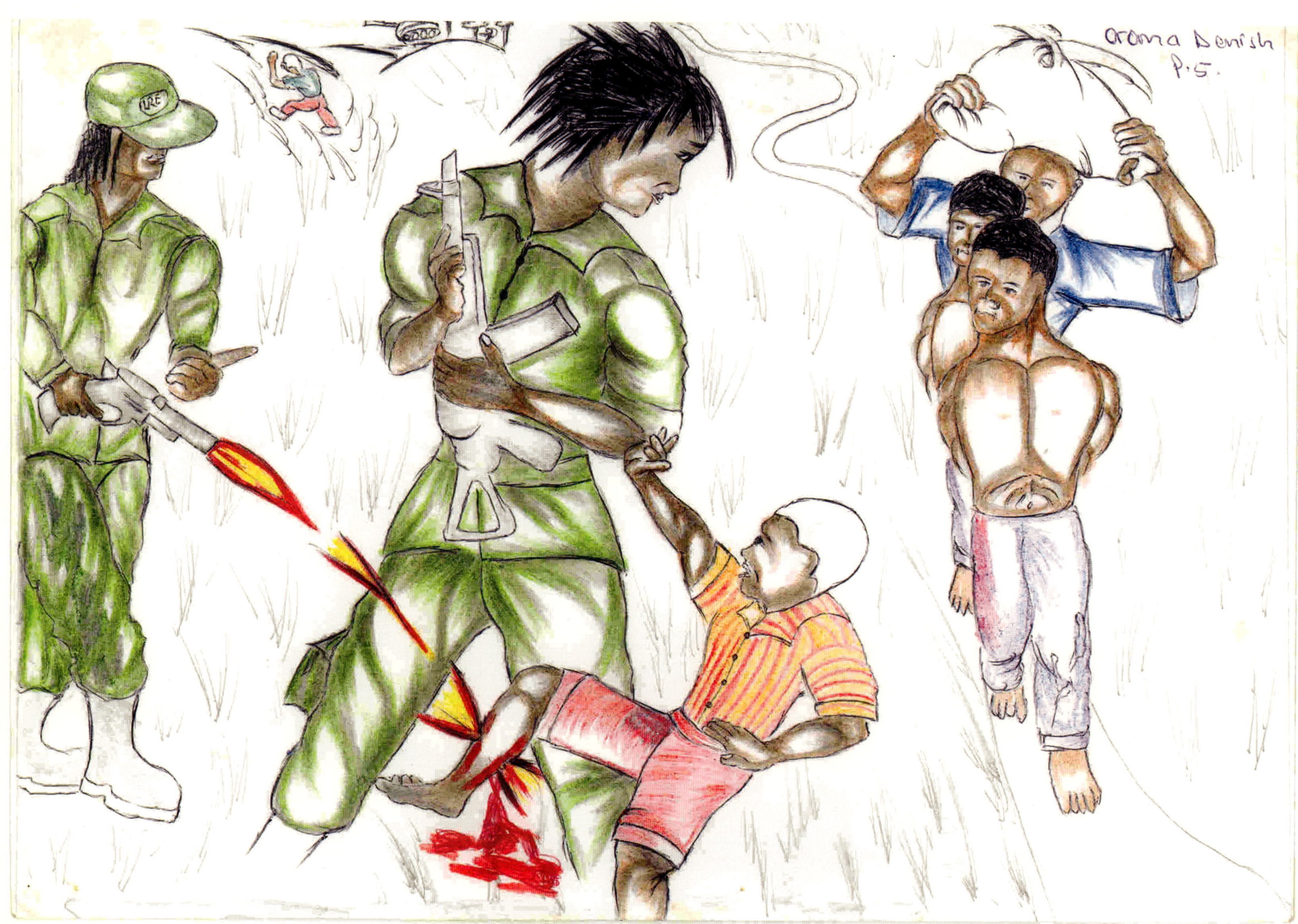
Oroma Denish
P.5.

Optional Protocol to the Convention on the Rights of the Child on the Involvement of Children in Armed Conflict

An abbreviated version

The States Parties to the present Protocol,

Encouraged by the overwhelming support for the Convention on the Rights of the Child, demonstrating the widespread commitment that exists to strive for the promotion and protection of the rights of the child,

Reaffirming that the rights of children require special protection, and calling for continuous improvement of the situation of children without distinction, as well as for their development and education in conditions of peace and security,

Disturbed by the harmful and widespread impact of armed conflict on children and the long-term consequences it has for durable peace, security and development,

Condemning the targeting of children in situations of armed conflict and direct attacks on objects protected under international law, including places that generally have a significant presence of children, such as schools and hospitals,

Noting the adoption of the Rome Statute of the International Criminal Court, in particular, the inclusion therein as a war crime, of conscripting or enlisting children under the age of 15 years or using them to participate actively in hostilities in both international and non-international armed conflicts,

Considering therefore that to strengthen further the implementation of rights recognized in the Convention on the Rights of the Child there is a need to increase the protection of children from involvement in armed conflict,

Noting that Article 1 of the Convention on the Rights of the Child specifies that, for the purposes of that Convention, a child means every human being below the age of 18 years unless, under the law applicable to the child, majority is attained earlier,

Convinced that an optional protocol to the Convention that raises the age of possible recruitment of persons into armed forces and their participation in hostilities will contribute effectively to the implementation of the principle that the best interests of the child are to be a primary consideration in all actions concerning children,

Condemning with the gravest concern the recruitment, training and use within and across national borders of children in hostilities by armed groups distinct from the armed forces of a State, and recognizing the responsibility of those who recruit, train and use children in this regard,

Recalling the obligation of each party to an armed conflict to abide by the provisions of international humanitarian law,

Bearing in mind that conditions of peace and security based on full respect of the purposes and principles contained in the Charter and observance of applicable human rights instruments are indispensable for the full protection of children, in particular during armed conflicts and foreign occupation,

Recognizing the special needs of those children who are particularly vulnerable to recruitment or use in hostilities contrary to the present Protocol owing to their economic or social status or gender,

Mindful of the necessity of taking into consideration the economic, social and political root causes of the involvement of children in armed conflicts,

Convinced of the need to strengthen international cooperation in the implementation of the present Protocol, as well as the physical and psychosocial rehabilitation and social reintegration of children who are victims of armed conflict,

Encouraging the participation of the community and, in particular, children and child victims in the dissemination of informational and educational programmes concerning the implementation of the Protocol,

Have agreed as follows:

Article 1
States Parties shall take all feasible measures to ensure that members of their armed forces who have not attained the age of 18 years do not take a direct part in hostilities.

Article 2
States Parties shall ensure that persons who have not attained the age of 18 years are not compulsorily recruited into their armed forces.

Article 3
1. States Parties shall raise the minimum age for the voluntary recruitment of persons into their national armed forces from that set out in Article 38, paragraph 3, of the Convention on the Rights of the Child, taking account of the principles contained in

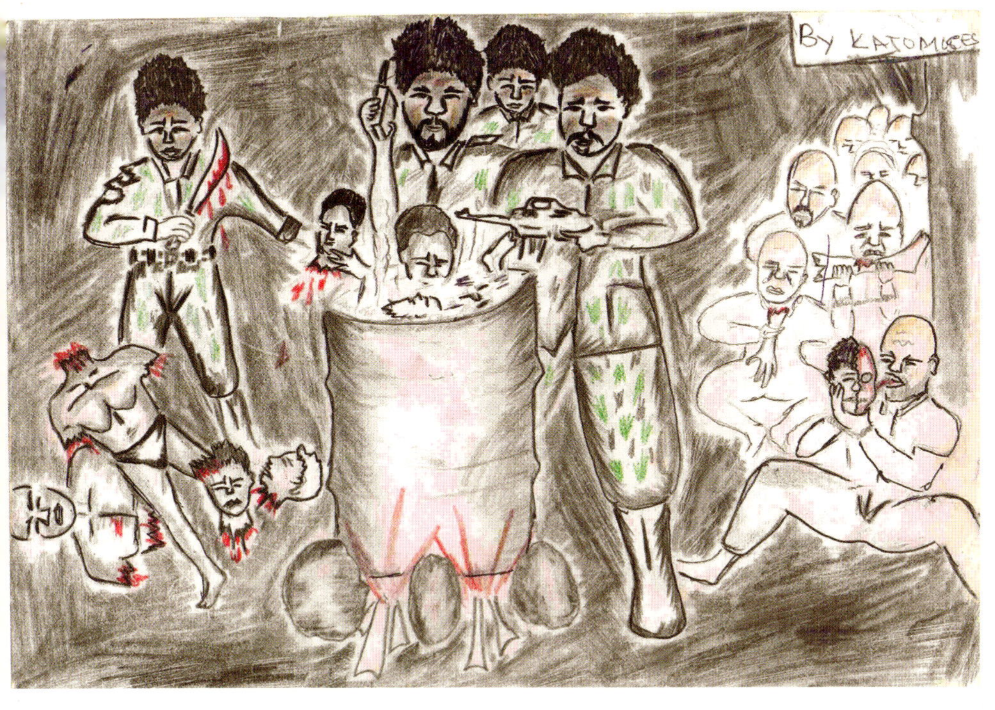
By KAJOMOSES

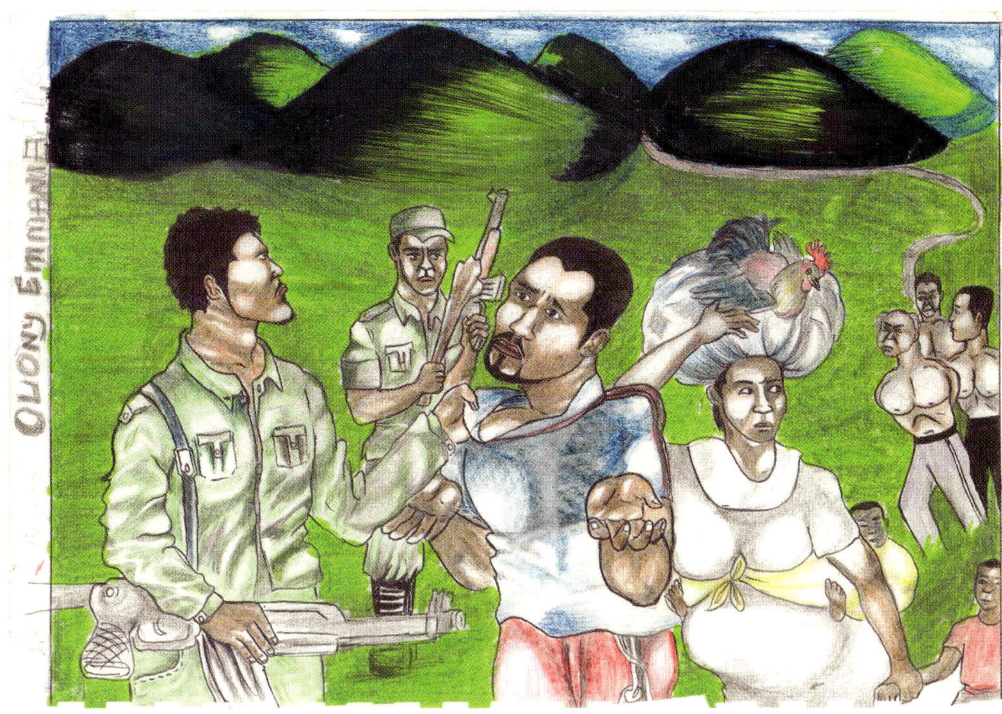
OLONY

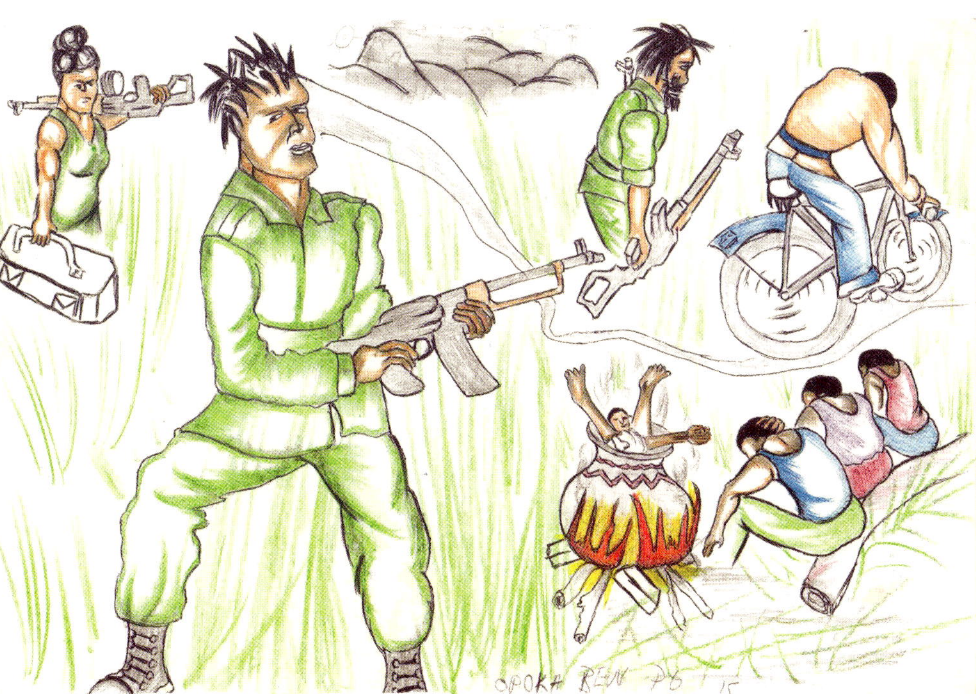
OPOKA BEN

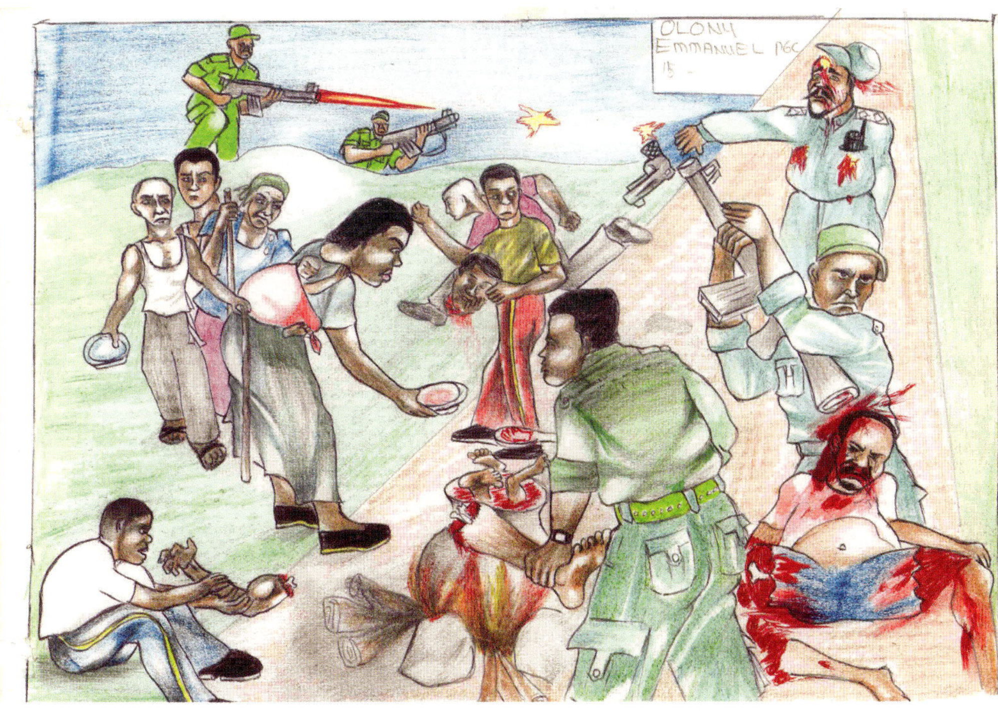
OLONY
EMMANUEL

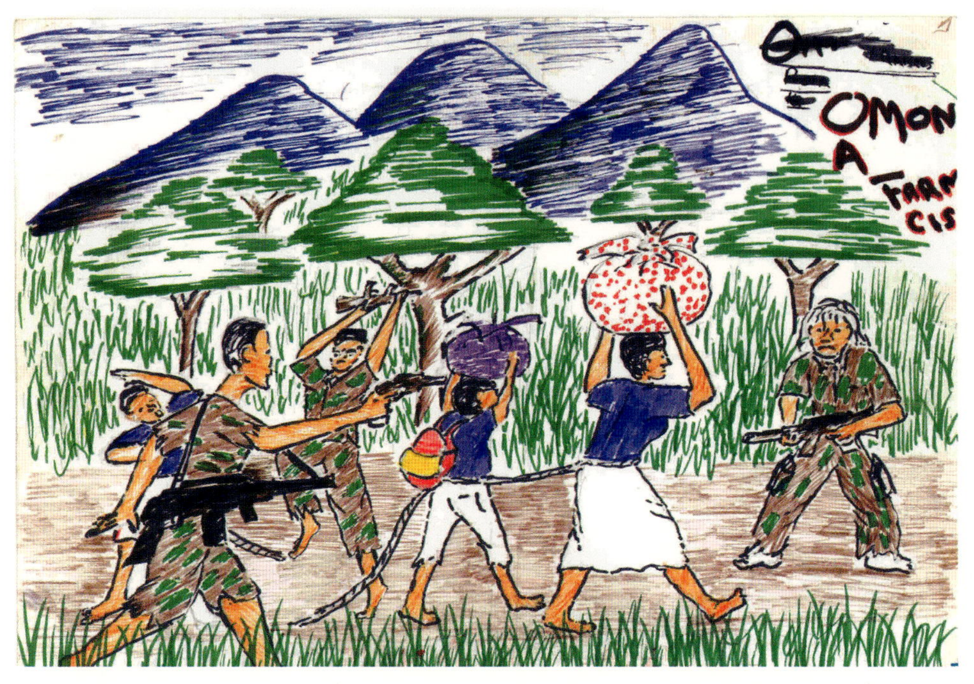
OMON
A

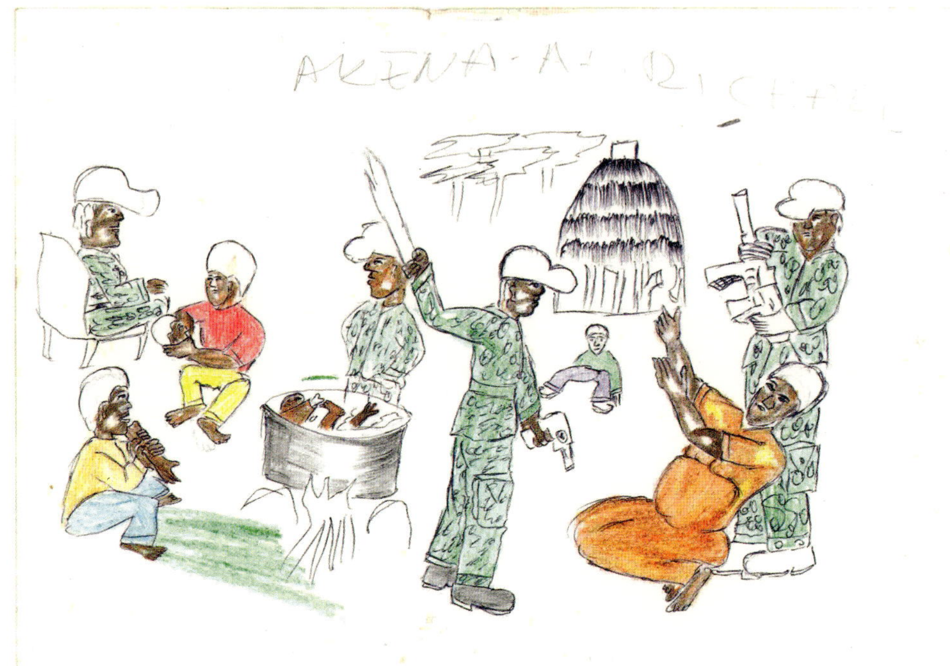
AKENA-A

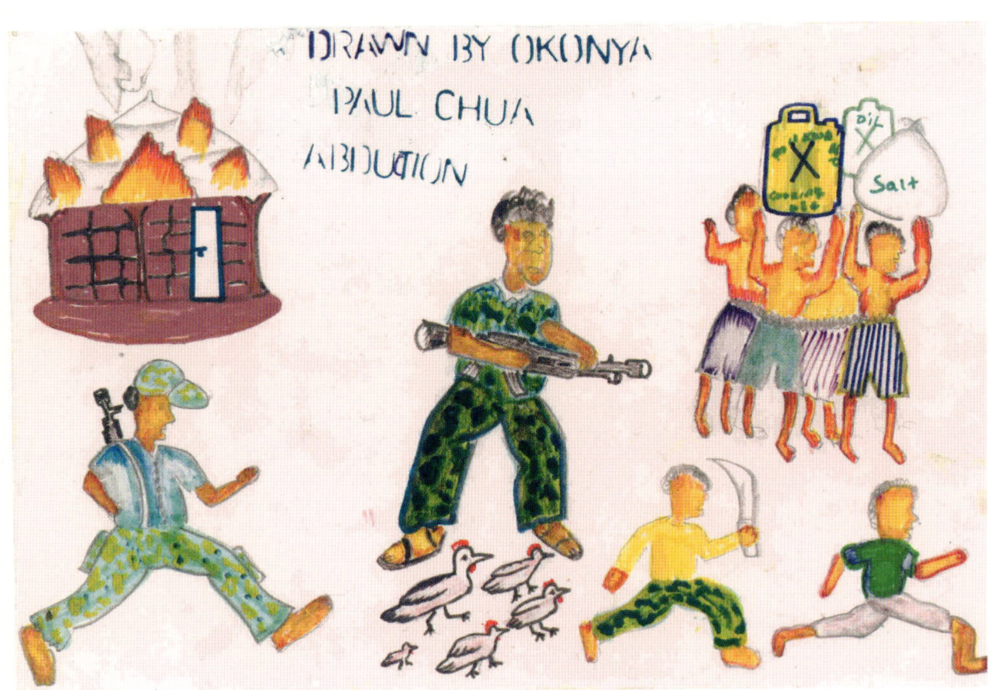
DRAWN BY OKONYA
PAUL CHUA
ABDUCTION
Oil
Salt

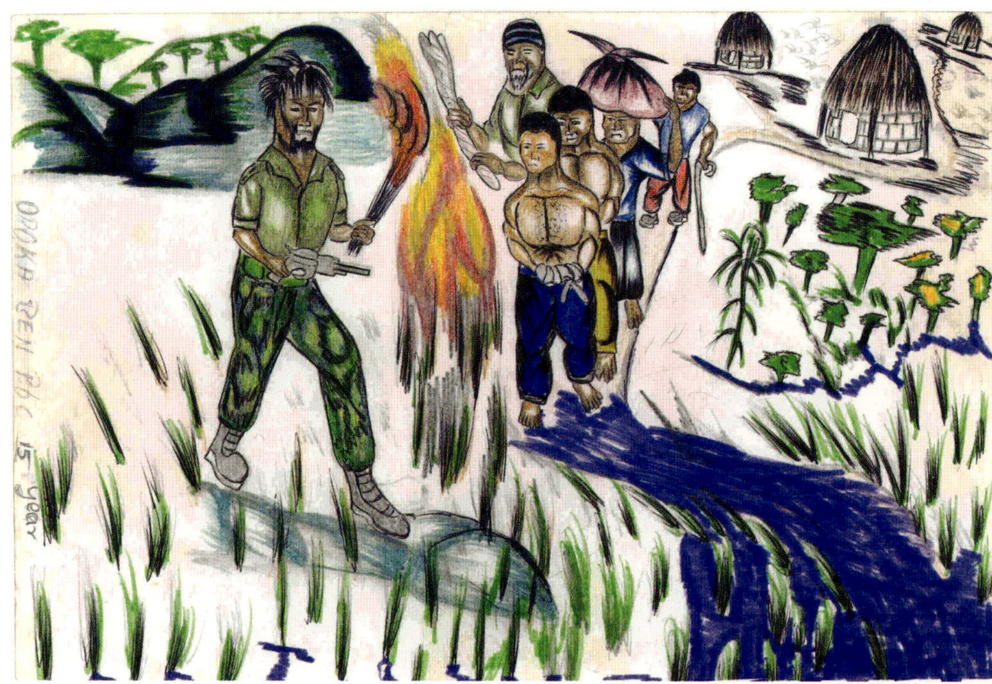
15 year

that article and recognizing that under the Convention persons under the age of 18 years are entitled to special protection.

2. Each State Party shall deposit a binding declaration upon ratification of or accession to the present Protocol that sets forth the minimum age at which it will permit voluntary recruitment into its national armed forces and a description of the safeguards it has adopted to ensure that such recruitment is not forced or coerced.

3. States Parties that permit voluntary recruitment into their national armed forces under the age of 18 years shall maintain safeguards to ensure, as a minimum, that:

(a) Such recruitment is genuinely voluntary;

(b) Such recruitment is carried out with the informed consent of the person's parents or legal guardians;

(c) Such persons are fully informed of the duties involved in such military service;

(d) Such persons provide reliable proof of age prior to acceptance into national military service.

5. The requirement to raise the age in paragraph 1 of the present article does not apply to schools operated by or under the control of the armed forces of the States Parties, in keeping with articles 28 and 29 of the Convention on the Rights of the Child.

Article 4

1. Armed groups that are distinct from the armed forces of a State should not, under any circumstances, recruit or use in hostilities persons under the age of 18 years.

2. States Parties shall take all feasible measures to prevent such recruitment and use, including the adoption of legal measures necessary to prohibit and criminalize such practices.

3. The application of the present article shall not affect the legal status of any party to an armed conflict.

Article 5

Nothing in the present Protocol shall be construed as precluding provisions in the law of a State Party or in international instruments and international humanitarian law that are more conducive to the realization of the rights of the child.

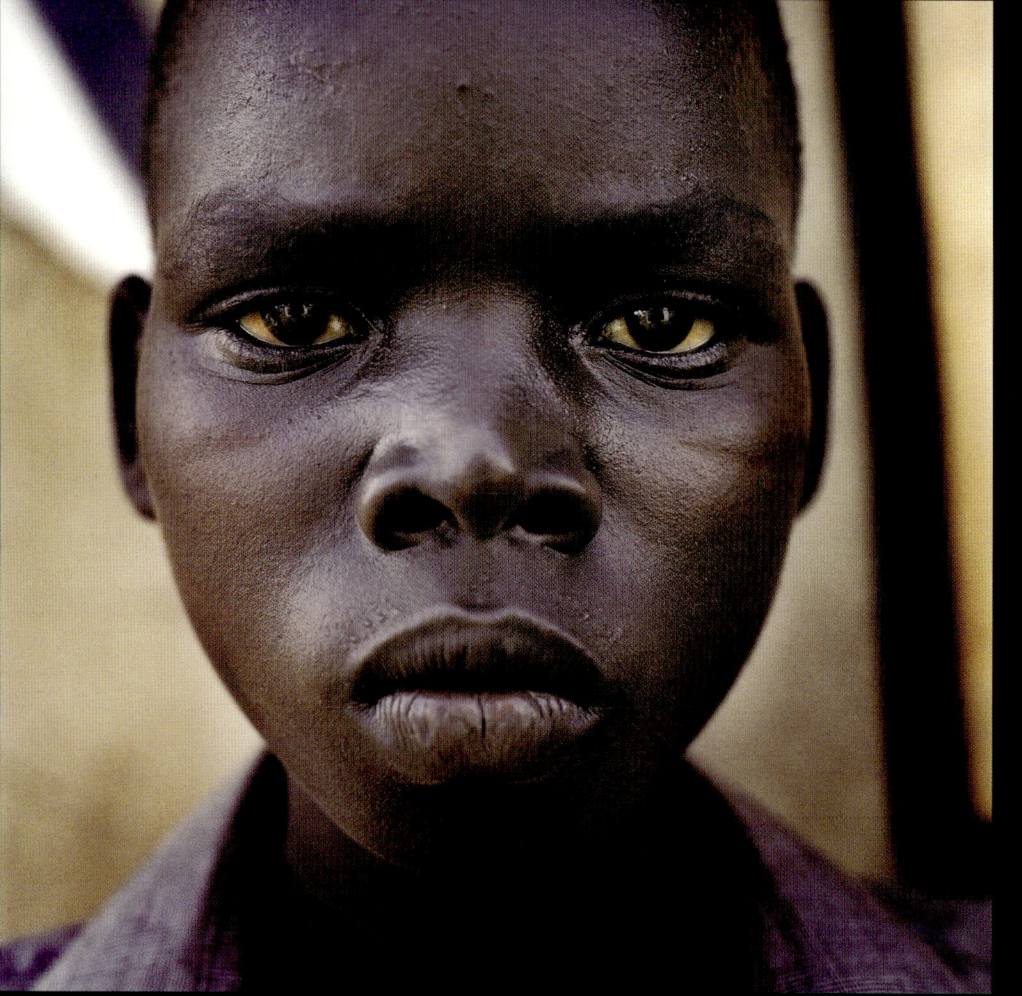

A 14-year-old Ugandan boy who was abducted and he
for two years by the Lord's Resistance Army (LRA) reb
He escaped after the LRA's hideout was destroyed by th
UPDF. Photograph by Chris de Bode/Panos

Preface

Children have been used as soldiers in armed conflict for hundreds of years. In the thirteenth century, thousands of children, many of them barely 12 years old, left their homes to march in the Children's Crusade. Sadly, the problem of child combatants is amply evident throughout the world today—and not just in Africa. Colombia, Guatemala, El Salvador, Nepal, Sri Lanka, Burma, Palestine, Afghanistan, Uganda, Sierra Leone, and the Congo are all represented in the images in this book.

The contributing photographers are talented visionaries whose work speaks for itself. They have ventured to the remote and dangerous places where child soldiers live in order to bring this story of injustice to the world. Through their images, they have become the messengers of a crime that could otherwise be easily ignored. They invite us to consider realms far removed from our own, ones that we could not bear to see our own children inhabit. These photos are drawn from recent and current conflicts. The children's names have been changed to protect them from reprisals and ostracization.

As Under-Secretary-General for Children and Armed Conflict, Radhika Coomaraswamy stated in her address to the Security Counsel in February 2008, "No one who has looked into the eyes of a child soldier can be at peace unless we rid this world of this scourge. No one who has held the hand of a young girl who has suffered multiple rapes can ever forget their duty to work for the protection of the vulnerable."

While the phenomenon of the child soldier is not new, its contemporary incarnation is especially chilling. The story these images tell is one of children manipulated by war criminals and subjected to unspeakable violence and abuse. Their faces depict the reality of a childhood lost. Instead of the frivolity and joy—or even the defiance and rebellion—of childhood, we see the deadly seriousness of the machinery of death in the hands of teenagers. Who will see past the grim confidence, the bravado, and the swagger to their origination in terrifying abductions and coerced recruitments? Who will look beyond their rifles and remember them as children? Precisely because we think we value childhood more than our forebears in the thirteenth century did, the figure of the child dressed and outfitted for war is indeed a particularly modern obscenity.

Leora Kahn
New York, 2008

Introduction

by Luis Moreno-Ocampo, International Criminal Court Prosecutor

I am a prosecutor—the first Prosecutor of the International Criminal Court. My mandate is to investigate and prosecute the worst criminals worldwide, those responsible for genocide, crimes against humanity, and war crimes, including the crime of recruiting child soldiers.

I am a parent. If my children were abducted and turned into killers or sex slaves, I would want them back. I would do everything in my power to get them back. I would never stop.

Child soldiers. According to the statistics, there are up to 300,000 of them worldwide. In some countries, more than a third of them are little girls, used as soldiers and sex slaves, and offered to officers as rewards. They are called "brides." Taken away from home, from their schools, they are plunged into the darkest recesses of humanity.

Child soldiers. Not playing at war. Learning to kill at twelve. For most of them, there will be no road back to normality. There will be only a descent into a nightmare where dying and putting to death, where raping and being raped, are normal.

Child soldiers. Lost children.

In Uganda and the Democratic Republic of the Congo, men like Joseph Kony, leader of the Lord's Resistance Army, have abducted children as young as six and transformed them into killers. "My brother begged them to take him instead of me," said one witness. "I was six. He was twelve. They killed him in front of me. From then on, I did whatever they said: burned people alive, killed babies because they slowed down their mothers."

Yet when arrest warrants were issued against Kony and his accomplices, and I went to states asking for their assistance in making the arrests, I was told that there were ongoing negotiations with the accused. I was told I needed to find them an exit. I was asked to withdraw the warrants.

An exit. More than their victims ever had, more than those children ever dreamed of. The criminals who use child soldiers take everything away from them, including their dreams.

For the criminals, exit strategies, amnesty, pardon. For the children, nothing. It has been seen before, of course. For centuries, criminals have been rewarded with power sharing, immunities, and golden exiles.

And the frustration and despair of victims, especially at the glee of perpetrators celebrating their impunity with yet more crimes, have fueled violence for generation after generation.

As the Prosecutor of the International Criminal Court, I will do everything in my power not to let it happen again. I will not let it happen in the DRC, or in Uganda. We as citizens must ask political leaders not to look away. Indifference is no longer an option.

Using children to fight adult wars is not a cultural practice. It is not a byproduct of war. It is not the sad but inescapable consequence of poverty. It is a terrible crime with clearly established codes. It involves terrorizing and abducting young children, putting them through brutal rites of initiation, and forcing them to kill community members, sometimes even family members, or be executed.

The list is long of armies, guerillas, and liberation movements that enlist children. Let our message to them be loud and clear. The story of Charles Taylor, former president of Liberia, prosecuted by the Special Court for Sierra Leone, the story of Thomas Lubanga Dyilo, former militia leader in the Ituri District of DRC, prosecuted by the International Criminal Court, must be told throughout the world. They were leaders, unassailable. They abused and recruited children to fight their wars. They ended up in court. They ended up in cells in the Hague. Joseph Kony will join them one day, as will the others. We are a permanent court. We will wait.

But the victims cannot wait. In one of the essays in this book, we learn about a boy so traumatized by his experience as a soldier that he began to have nightmares. "The man I killed," he says, "his spirit comes to me at night and asks, 'Why did you do this to me?'"

Recruiting child soldiers is a crime, and will be prosecuted.

Luis Moreno-Ocampo has been the Prosecutor of the International Criminal Court since its formation in 2002.

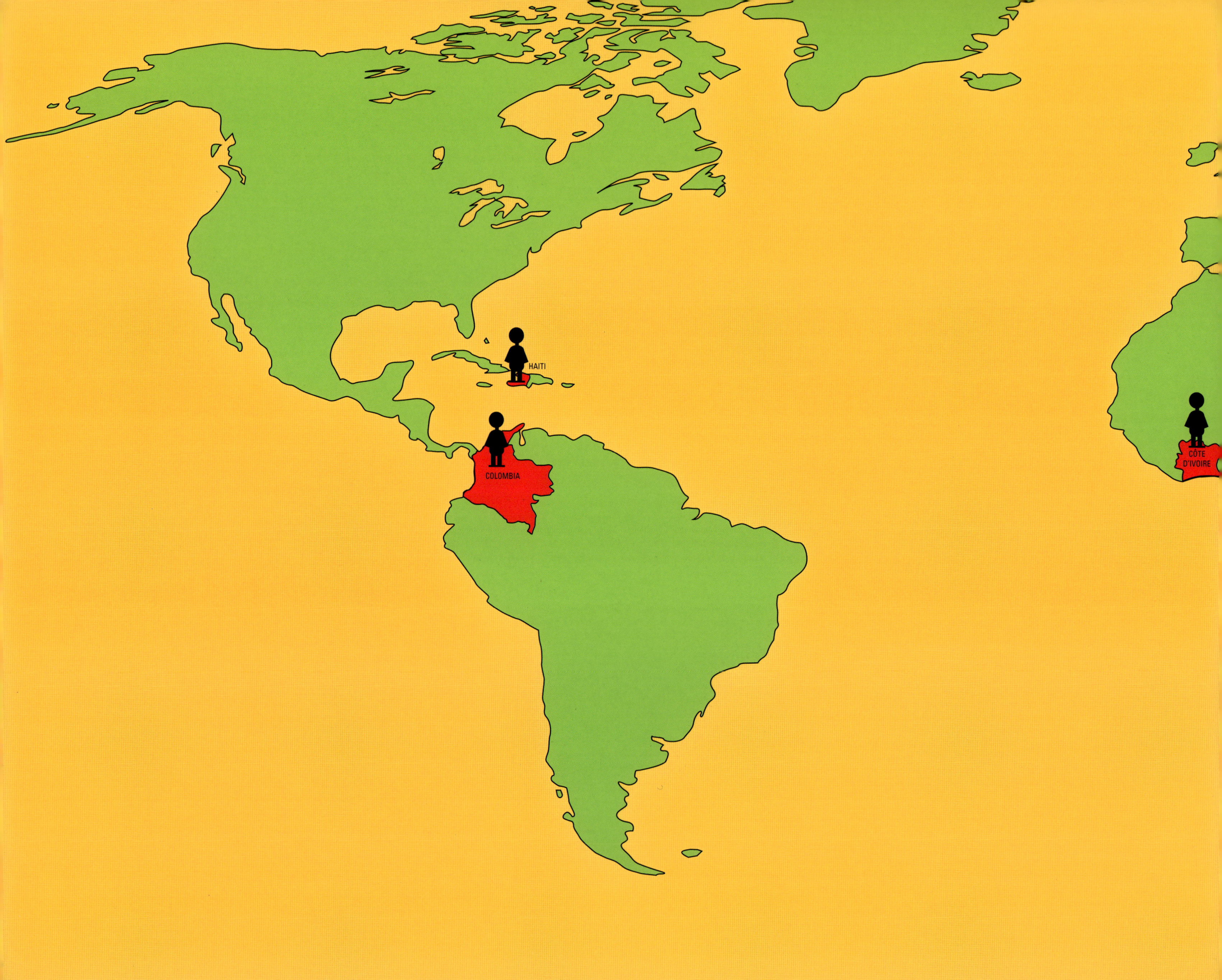
HAITI
COLOMBIA
CÔTE
D'IVOIRE

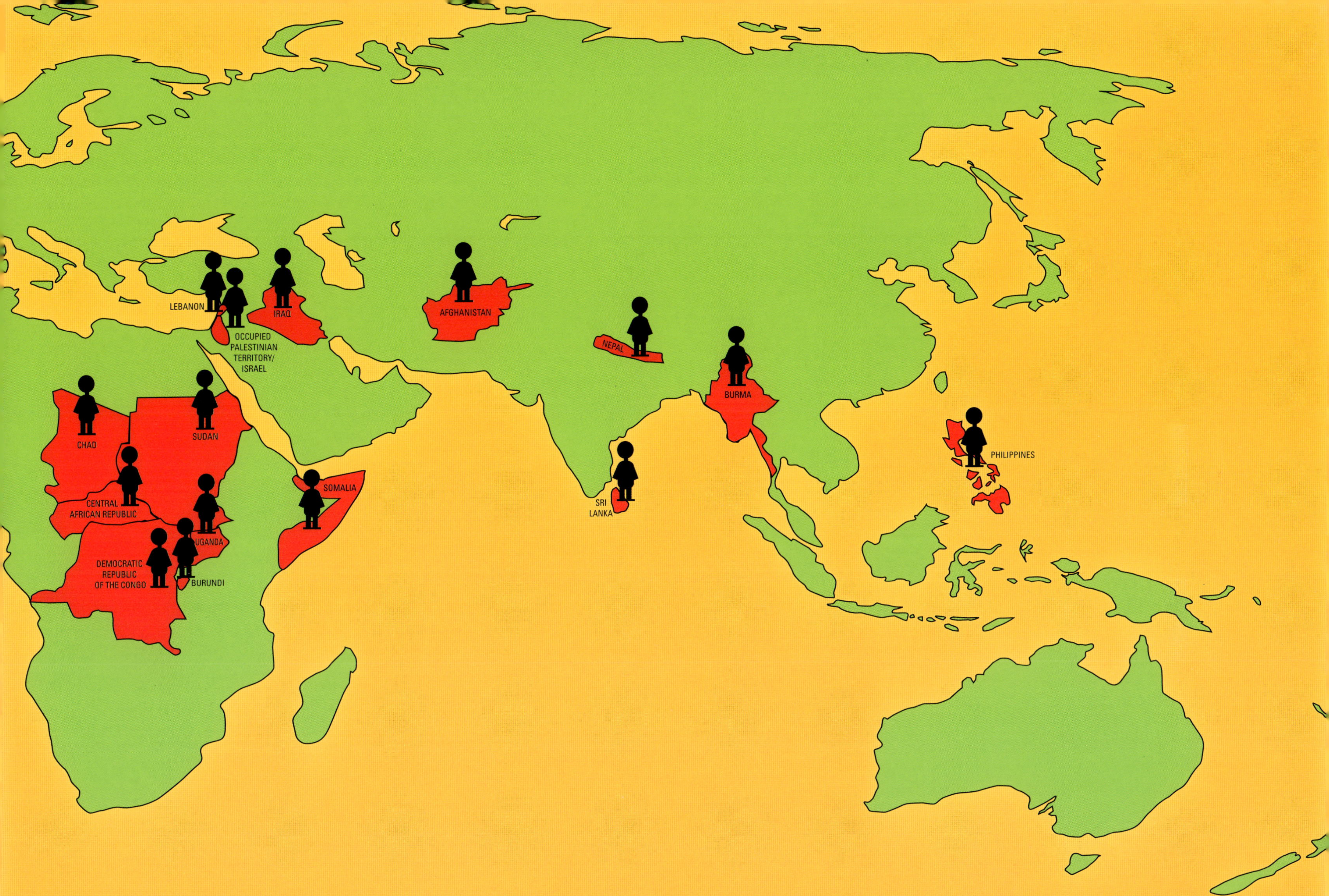

World Map of Children Affected by Armed Conflict

Based on the violations against children in situations of concern as covered in the Secretary-General's Annual Report on Children and Armed Conflict (A/62/609 S/2007/757, December 21, 2007), including recruitment or use of children as soldiers, attacks against schools or hospitals, denial of humanitarian access for children, abduction of children, and rape and other grave sexual abuse of children.

the americas: colombia

"I joined the guerilla when I was ten years old. I wanted to serve in an armed group; it appealed to me. After five years I withdrew. I was tired—very, very tired. We had to fight every single day and it was very tough. One day we were fighting in the bush. All of a sudden a grenade or something like that landed near my feet. I tried to pick it up and throw it away, but it exploded. My comrades left me for dead on the battlefield. I got lucky; normally you wouldn't survive this. I was found by the government military and they took me to a hospital in the city. After some time I recovered. It was a miracle.

After I left the hospital I was brought over to a shelter for rehabilitation. I tried it for six months. It didn't suit me, and I decided to join the paramilitary. I went back to the armed groups. I joined them for two years and had a reasonably good life; I earned money and wasn't tortured. But I had a very difficult time getting away. I met some people and finally ended up in a criminal environment, where a gang operated in the city. During that period I was addicted to drugs.

Over a period of time I have learned to live my own life. Now I can read and write.

I don't want to go back. I want to be myself and don't want to be discouraged.

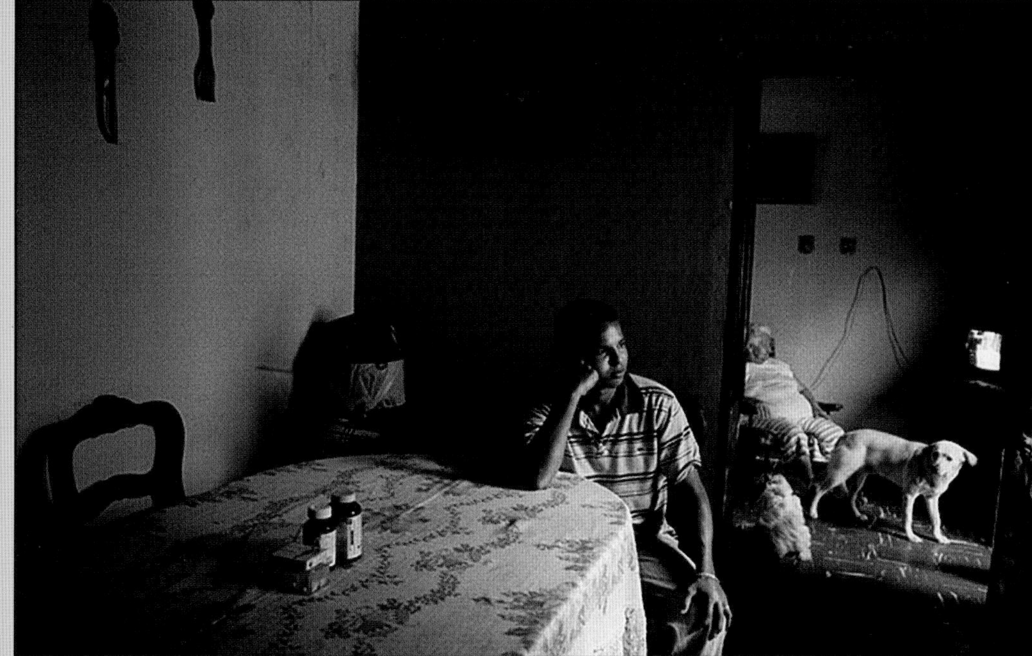

Photograph by Vincent van de Wijngaard

I want to leave this illegal way of life far behind.

I can't stop thinking about the past; deep inside it is always there. I don't see my parents often. Sometimes I am still scared of my former comrades, that they are searching for me and will kill me."

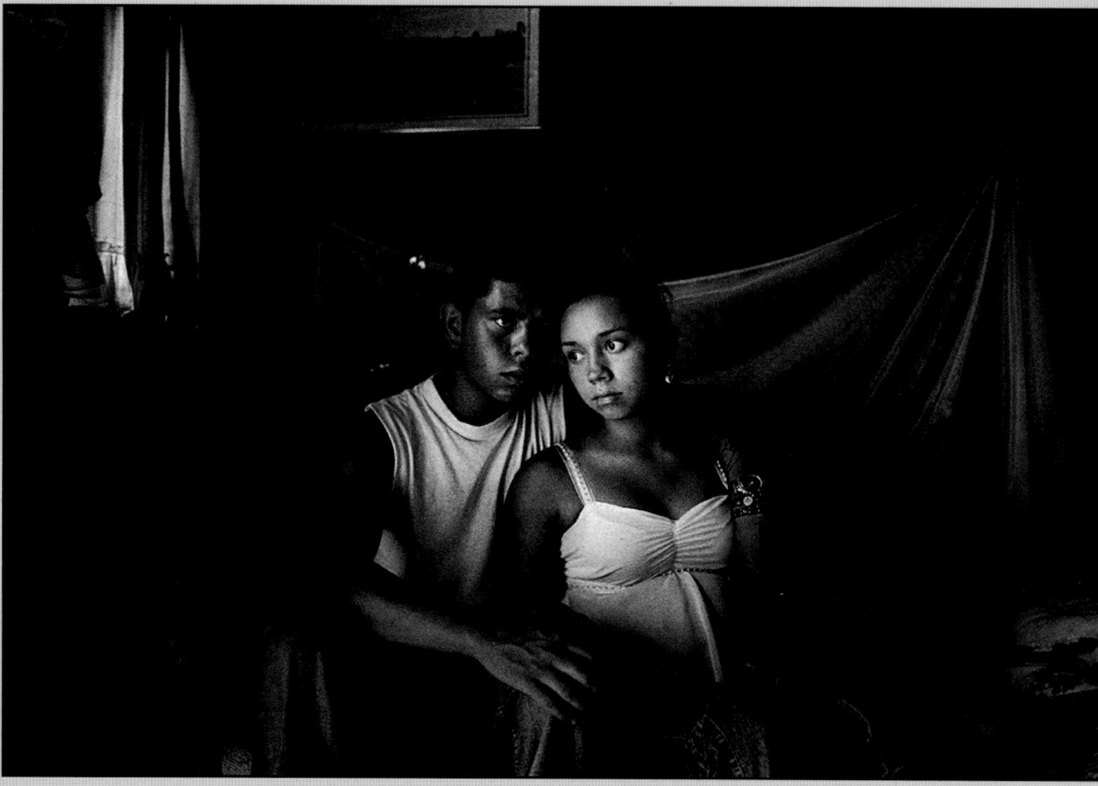

Paulo and Mercedes are former child soldiers who met in a rehabilitation center. They became a couple, and are expecting a child soon.

"I didn't want to fight anymore," says Mercedes about her last deployment. "But if they said to go to the front line, you had to go. We had to walk for days without getting any sleep or food. I was very sad when I had to see my friends die. Within the group I experienced war, hunger, and cold.

"One day, at the age of thirteen, I managed to escape. I was sent out as a patroller and all of a sudden I became desperate. I sat down and all I could do was cry. I looked out over the valley and I heard music. I stopped thinking. I started running down a narrow path and kept running."

Paulo insists at first that he was only hired by his military group to clean the floors. But when pressed by one of the shelter employees to talk about his time as a soldier, he concedes some brutal details. "Warfare is much more than just holding a gun," he says. "I also used explosives and mines; I blew up houses with families in them." He admits, however, to what he found so attractive about the job: "I like rifles. Having a rifle gives me a good feeling. I just love to hold them. When I had a rifle, I was in charge. I had a very good time with my friends. Sometimes I think of returning."

Paulo managed to escape one day while he was on guard. He ran for days, hiding in the rainforest south of Cali until he eventually reached a shelter. His former partners in battle searched for him; had they found him, he would undoubtedly have been killed.

Now, he looks at his pregnant girlfriend and remarks, "I am looking forward to my child." But he seems uncomfortable as he says the words, as though uncertain how a child is meant to be loved.

Above: Photograph by Vincent van de Wijngaard. Right: In Colombia, a girl stands at a hairdresser's with her gun. Photograph by Kadir van Lohuizen/Noor

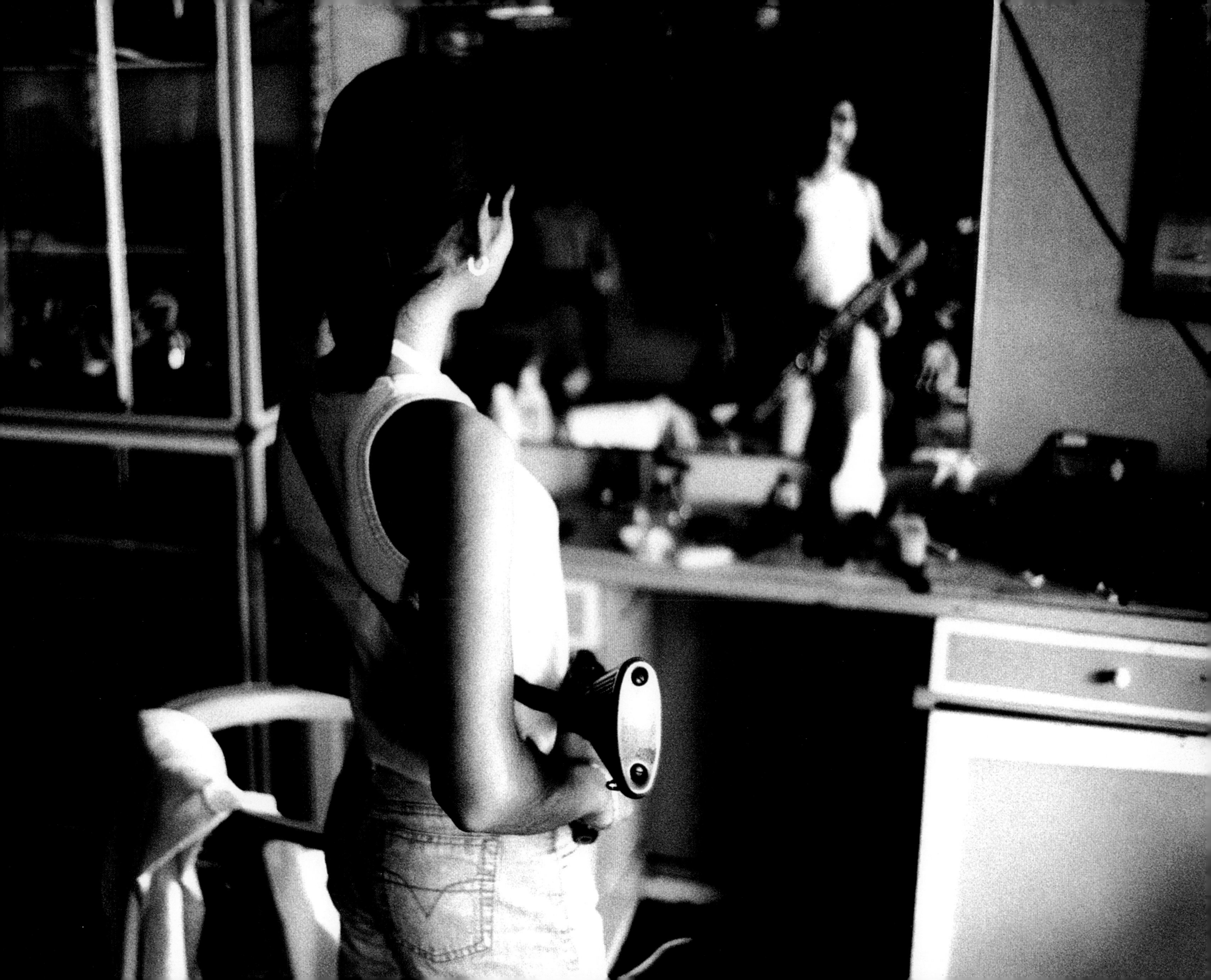

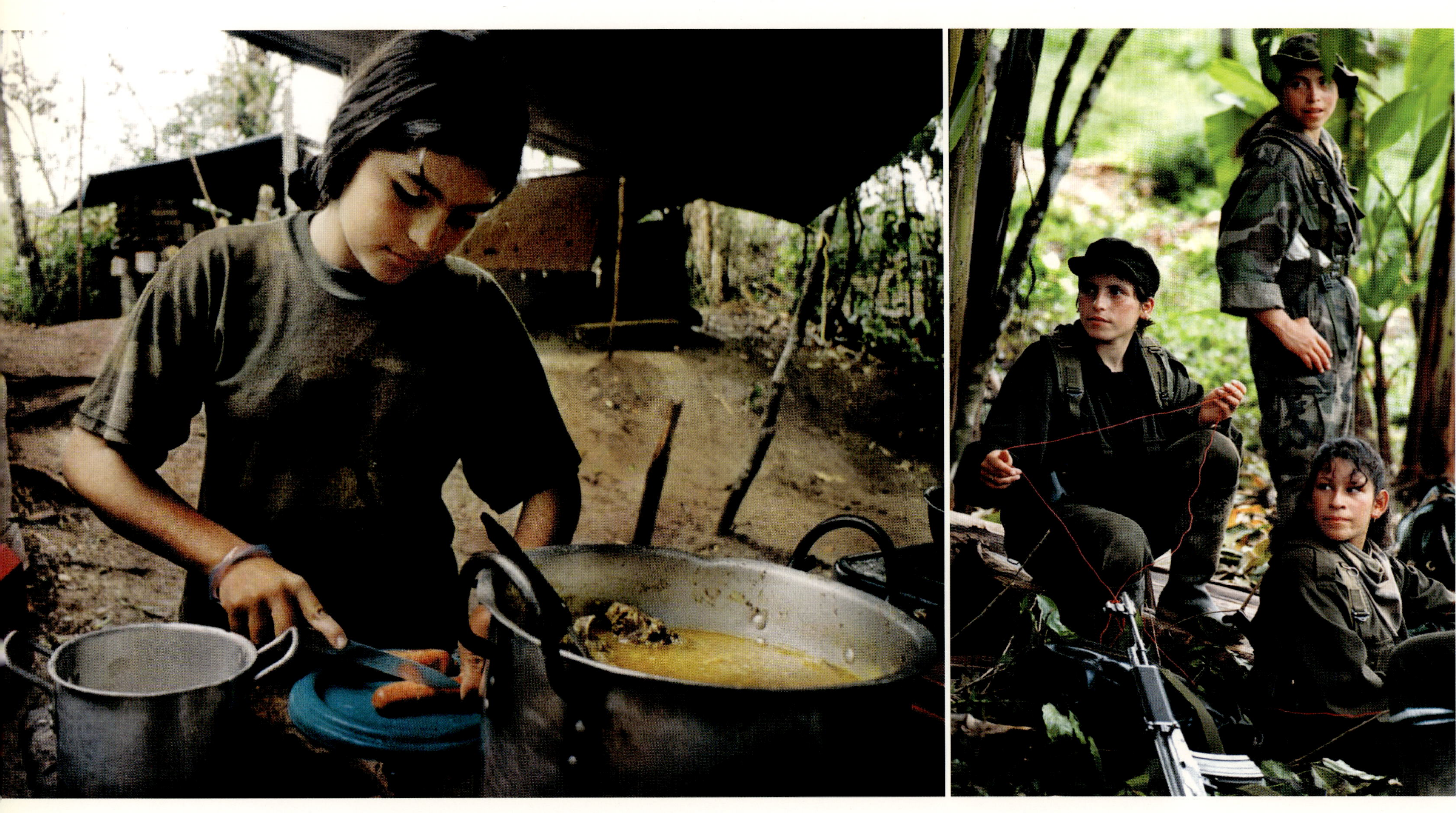

Above left: A young Revolutionary Armed Force of Colombia (FARC) rebel cooks with a camp stove at a rebel camp. Above right: Three members of the FARC at a camp near the rebel-controlled area. Right: Colombian rebels of the National Liberation Army (ELN) march in Arauca, northern Colombia. Photographs by Marcelo Salinas

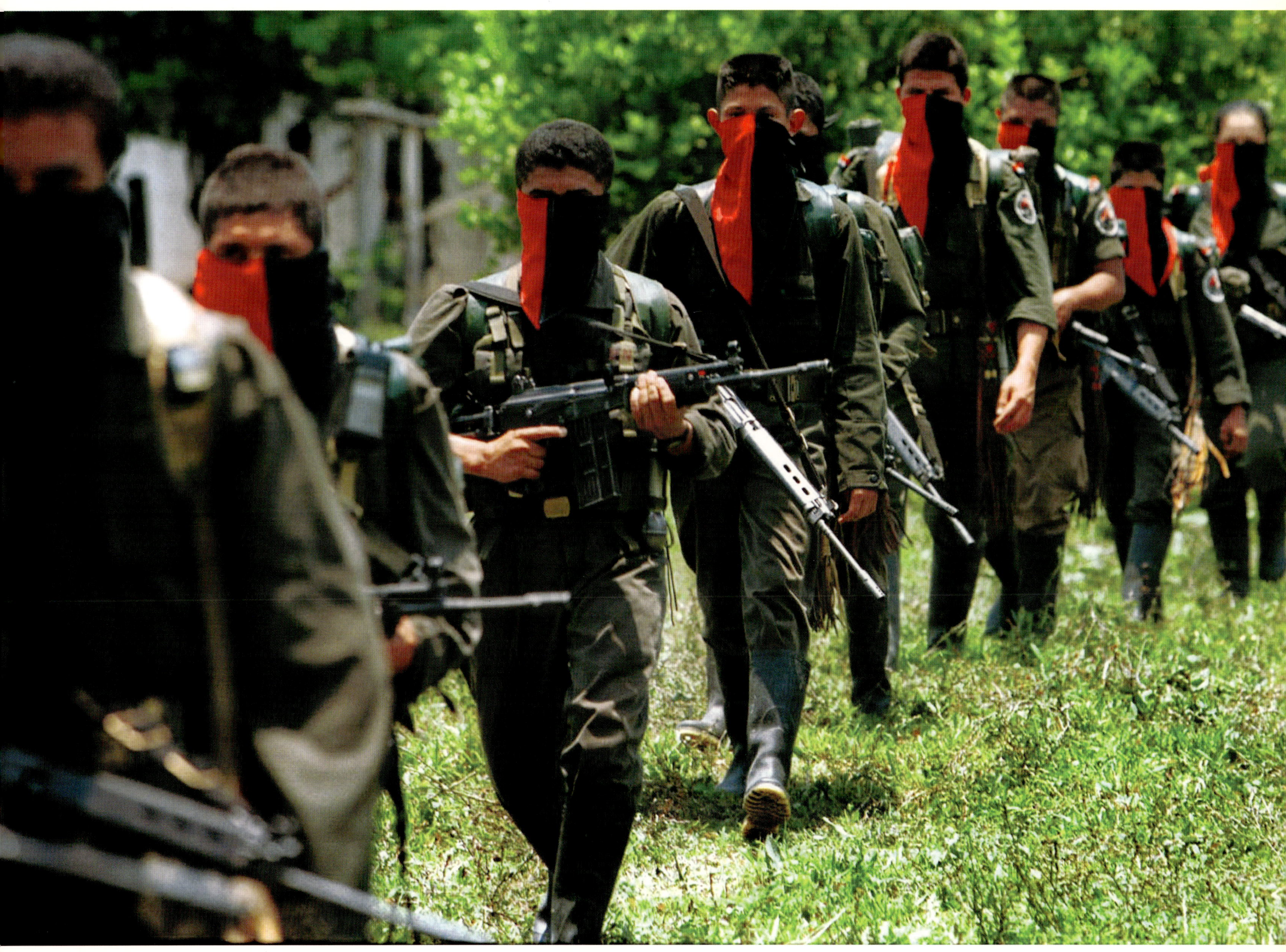

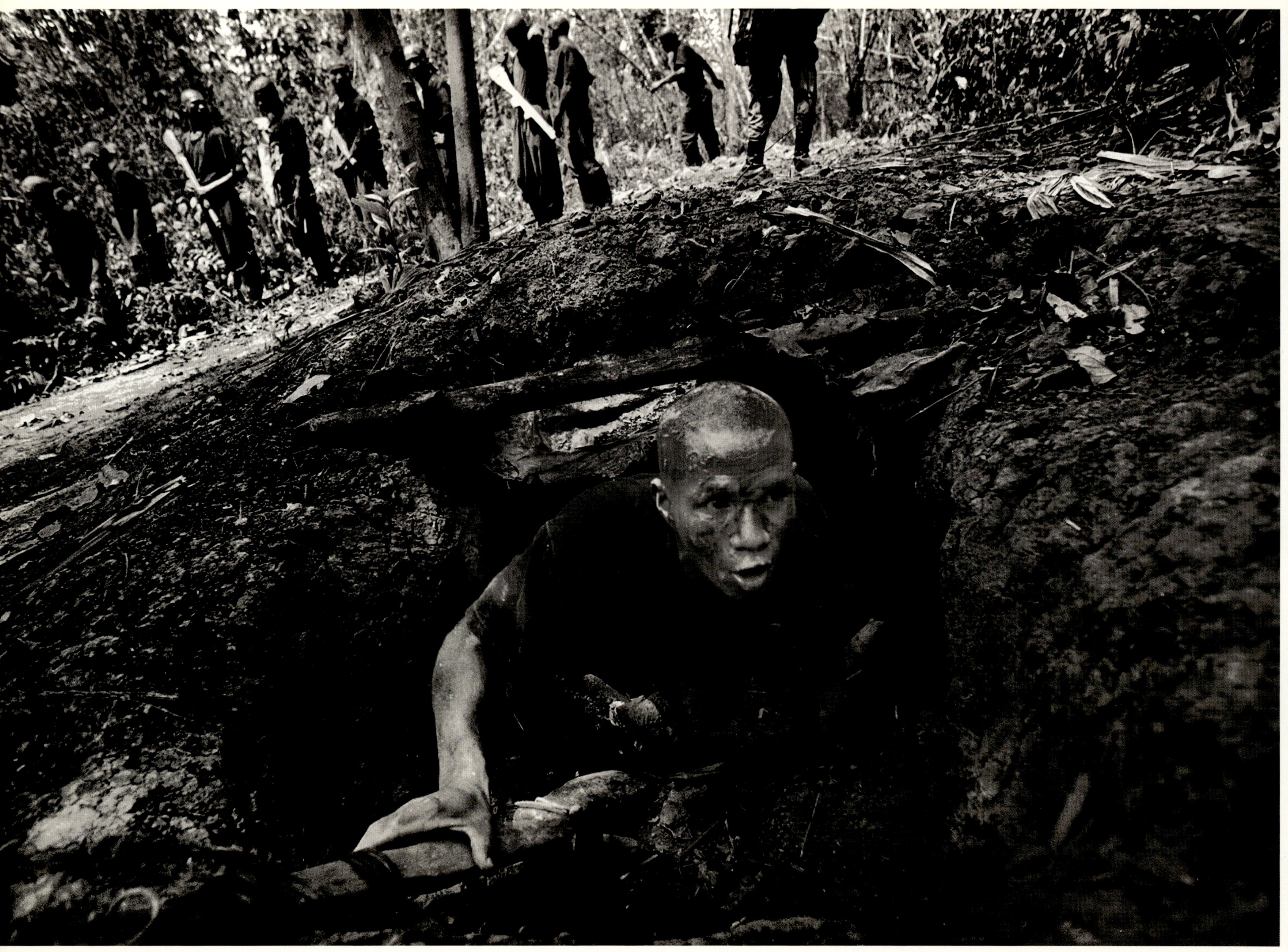

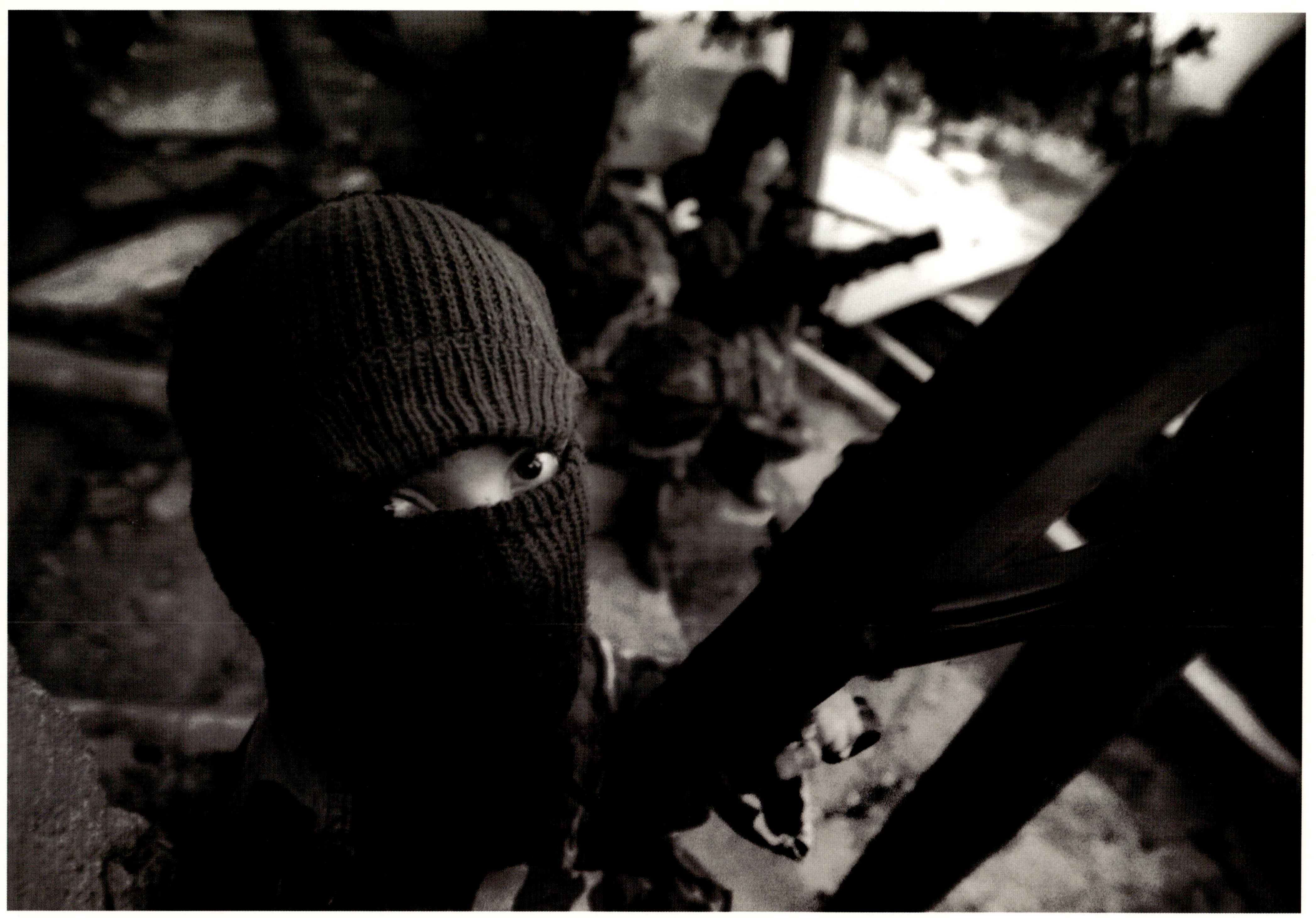

Left: A new recruit of the United Self-Defense Forces of Colombia (AUC) trains in a camp. Above: A member of the AUC patrols a neighborhood in Medellin. Photographs by Marcelo Salinas

the americas: guatemala and el salvador

Boy soldier rests with gun. Photograph by Miquel Dewever Plana/Agence VU

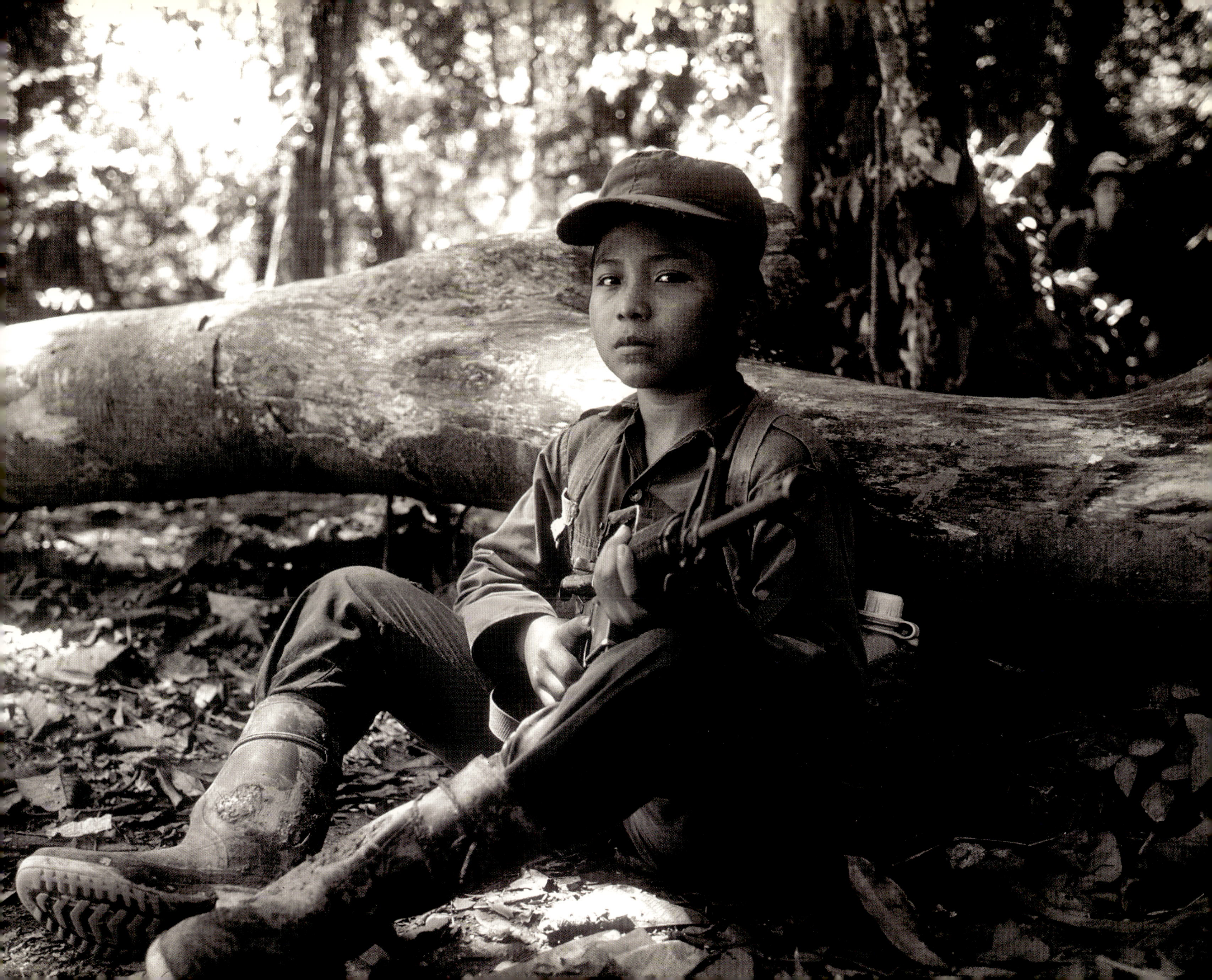

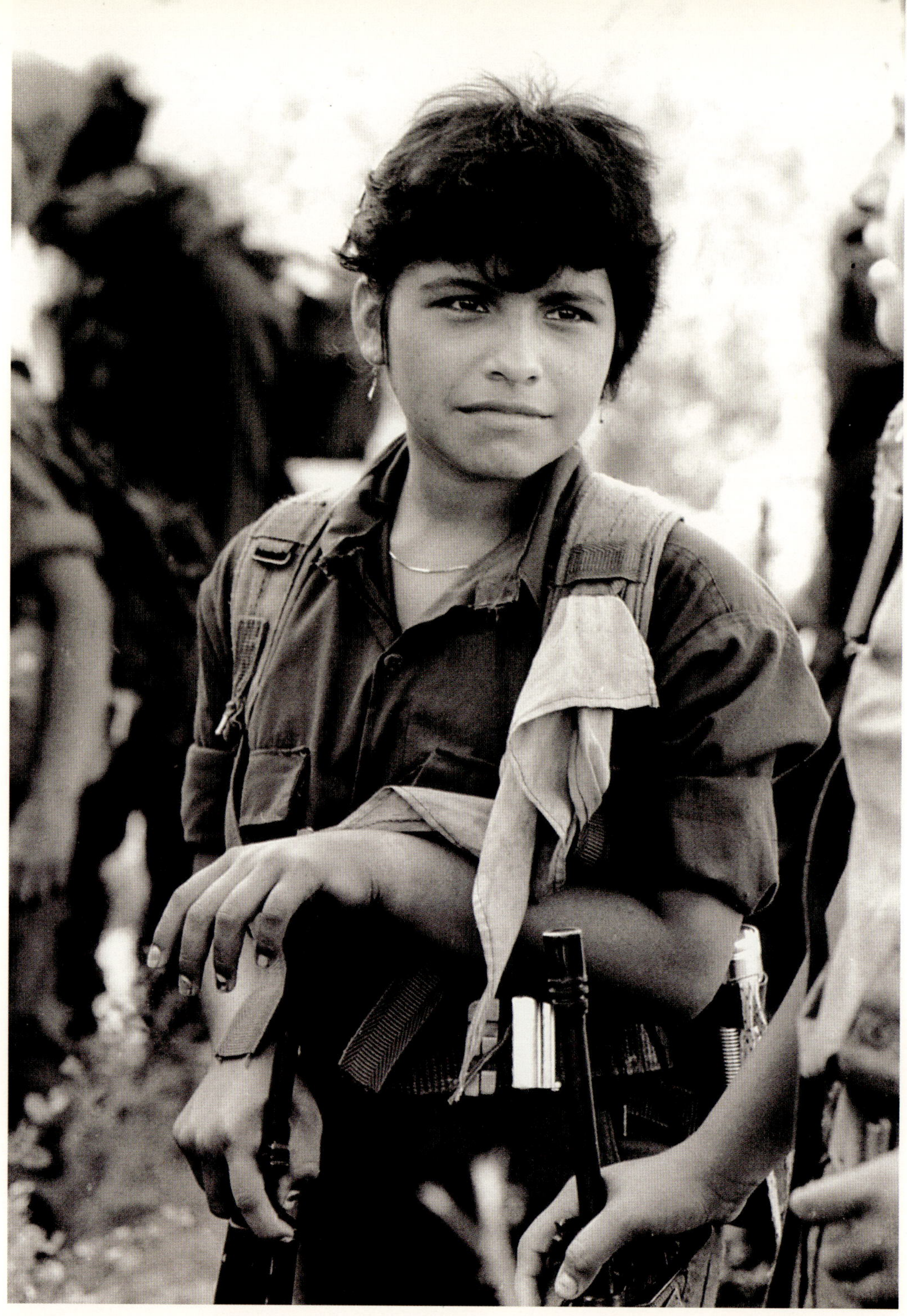

Above: A Farabundo Martí National Liberation Front (FMLN) girl soldier. Photograph by Rhodri Jones/Panos. Right: FMLN soldiers, some of them children, on patrol in the mountains. Photograph by Martin Adler/Panos

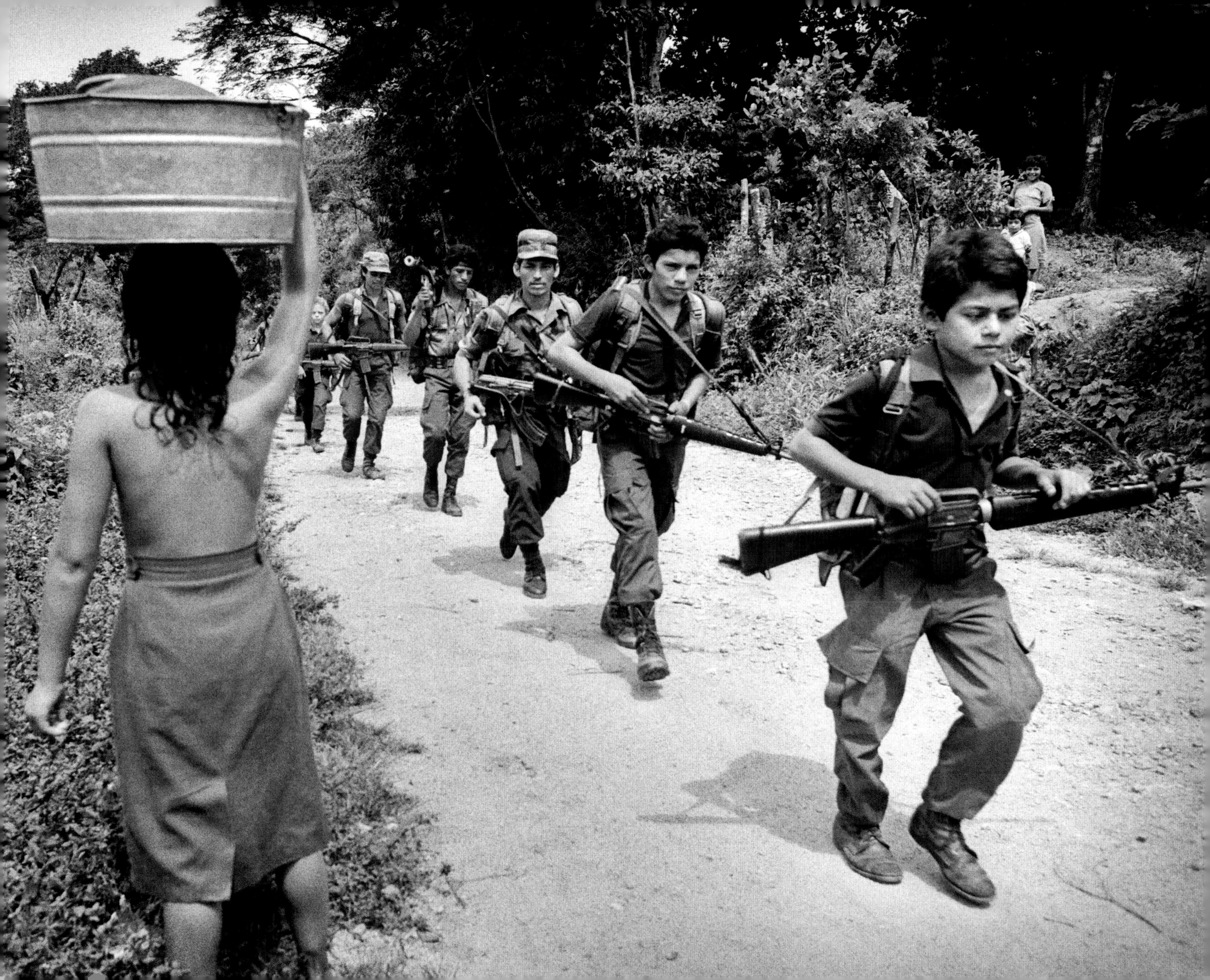

A 13-year-old FMLN Guatemalan girl fighter poses with her rifle next to graffiti. Photograph by Martin Adler/Panos

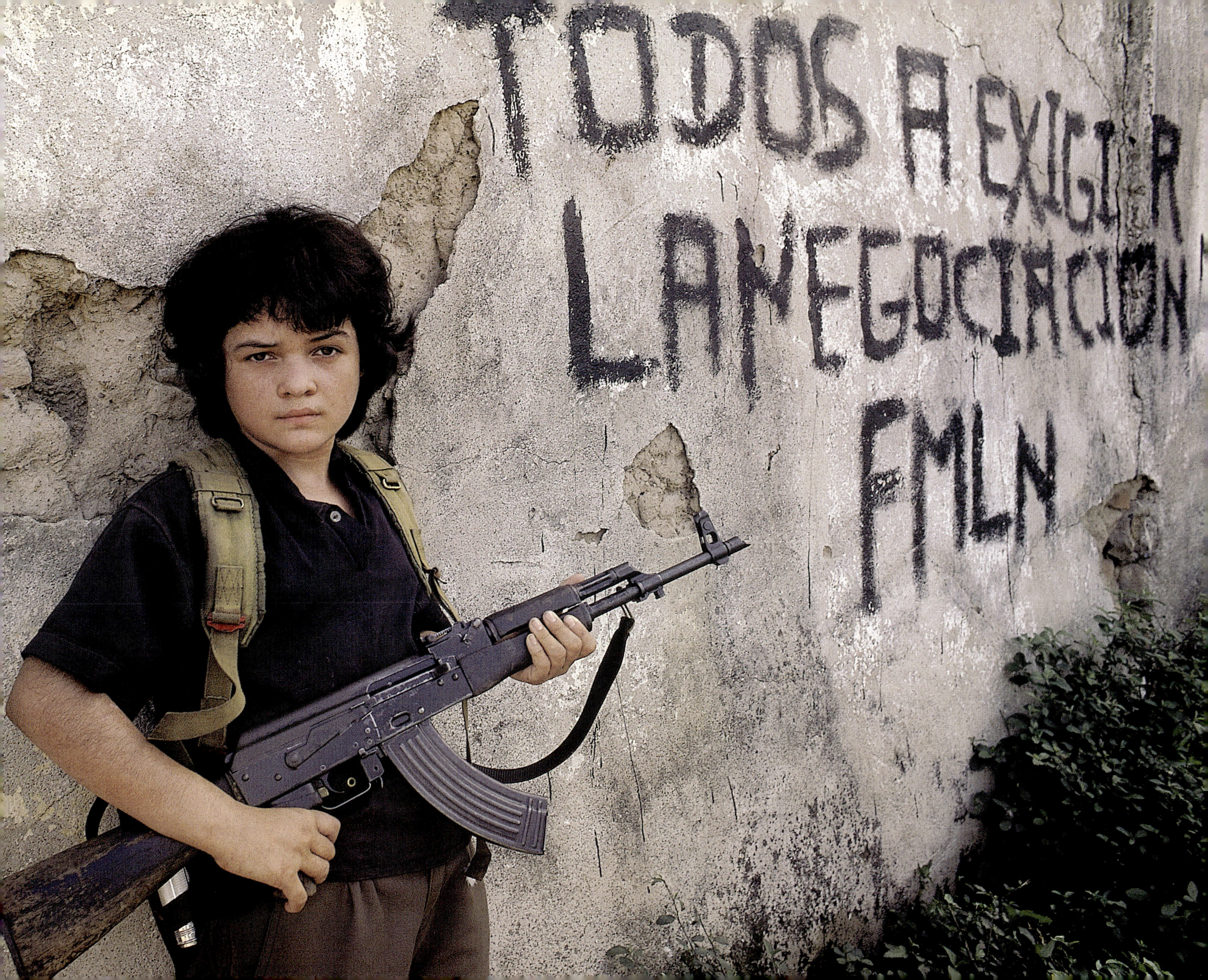
TODOS A EXIGIR
LANEGOCIACION
FMLN

Returning Childhood to Children: How We Can Stop War Criminals from Recruiting Children as Soldiers

Senator Richard J. Durbin

Of all the unspoken casualties of war, the use of children as soldiers is among the most heartbreaking and horrific.

Every day, hundreds of thousands of children are forced at gunpoint to surrender another day of their childhood. These boys and girls—some as young as seven or eight years old—are used as porters, sex slaves, and human mine detectors by state-run armies, paramilitaries, and guerrilla groups.

The use of child soldiers is not only morally repugnant, it is a war crime. And more than 110 countries, including the United States, have approved an international convention which sets the minimum age for compulsory recruitment of soldiers at 18.

Yet the use of child soldiers continues. Since 2001, children have been pressed into combat in at least 21 conflicts around the globe.

I chair the United States Senate's Subcommittee on Human Rights and the Law. Created in January 2007, it is the first committee in the more than 200-year history of the United States Congress dedicated to human rights as a matter of law, not simply a matter of morality.

One of the first hearings our subcommittee held, in April 2007, explored what the law can do to protect children who were forced to serve as soldiers.

Ishmael Beah, a former child soldier in Sierra Leone and author of the best-selling *A Long Way Gone: Memoirs of a Boy Soldier* (Farrar, Straus and Giroux, 2007) testified at the hearing and posed a moral challenge to all of us:

"When you go home tonight to your children, your cousins, and your grandchildren and watch them carrying out their various childhood activities, I want you to remember that at that same moment, there are countless children elsewhere who are being killed, injured, exposed to extreme violence, and forced to serve in armed groups, including girls who are raped (leading some to have the babies of commanders), all of them between the ages of eight and 17. As you watch your loved ones, those children you adore most, ask yourselves whether you would want these kinds of suffering for them. If you don't, then you must stop this from happening to other children around the world, whose lives and humanity are as important and of the same value as all children everywhere."

There are signs that the world is beginning to rise to this moral challenge. International courts have begun prosecuting those who use child soldiers.

In 2005, the International Criminal Court (ICC) issued arrest warrants for two commanders of the Lord's Resistance Army in Uganda—the ICC's first warrants ever for the enlistment of children as soldiers. The ICC's first prosecution is of the leader of a political group from the

Democratic Republic of Congo for forcing children to fight in the armed wing of his party.

In June 2007, the Special Court for Sierra Leone became the first international court to hand down convictions for the recruitment of child soldiers.

These prosecutions are important and positive developments. But the reality remains: war criminals around the world continue to use children to wage war. And they do so with virtual impunity because the ability of courts to prosecute those who recruit child soldiers is too limited.

As the first nation founded on the idea of human freedom as an inalienable right, I believe the United States has a special obligation to lead the effort to abolish the use of child soldiers worldwide. Sadly, however, as I write these words, recruiting and using child soldiers still does not violate any criminal or immigration law of the United States.

In the absence of any such laws, war criminals who have forced children into combat can find safe haven in the U.S. and our government has no power to prosecute them.

To close this loophole, I have introduced the Child Soldiers Accountability Act, which would allow the U.S. to prosecute anyone on U.S. soil who has recruited or used children as soldiers.

Governments that commit this crime must also be held accountable.

The U.S. State Department's 2006 Human Rights Report cites ten nations for using children as soldiers. Since 2001, nine of those ten nations have received military aid from the U.S. government.

The Child Soldiers Prevention Act, which I have also introduced, would bar such aid. The U.S. ought to stop funding and training the militaries of nations that use, or tolerate the use of, child soldiers. Period. To do otherwise would be to support the crime that we publicly condemn.

When we ask ourselves the question Ishmael Beah posed—would we want our children or grandchildren to endure the pain and suffering that Mr. Beah and other child soldiers have faced?—we all agree, the answer is no.

We all agree that exploiting children as soldiers is morally wrong and must be stopped. But neither moral suasion nor international agreements have been sufficient. We must close the loopholes in our laws, and prosecute those who violate the law for the war criminals they are.

Richard J. Durbin is a senior senator from Illinois.

asia: sri lanka

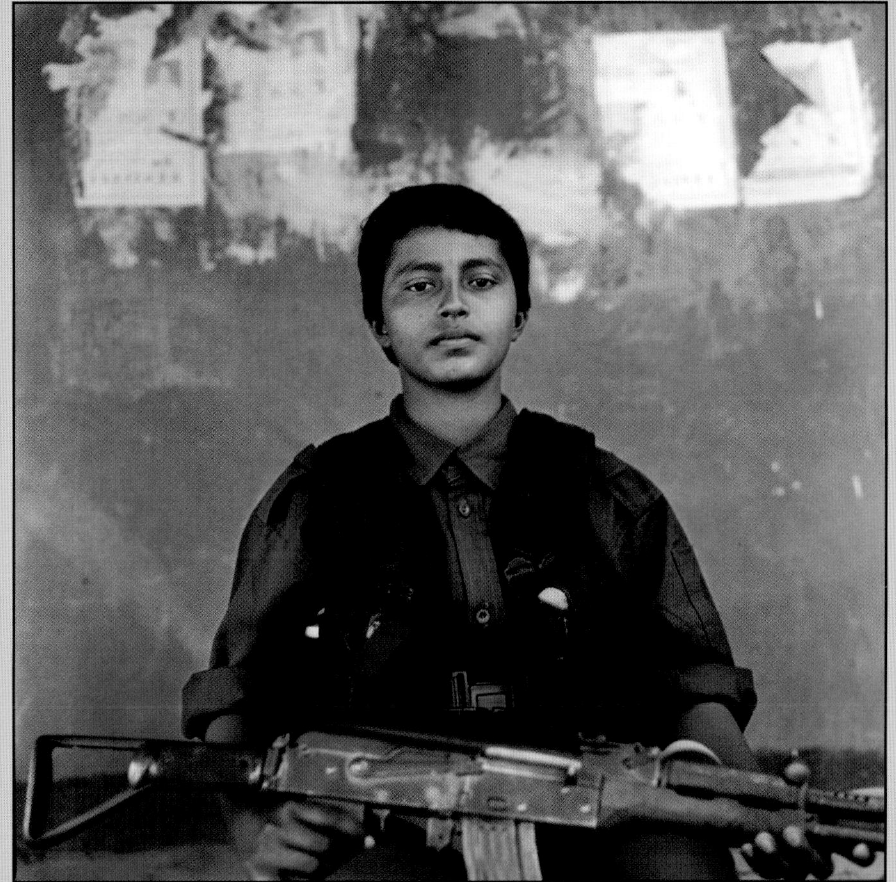

Photograph by Olivier Pin Fat/Agence VU

Selina is a 17-year-old Tamil Tiger who is fighting with the Karuna renegade faction. She became a Tiger four years ago after government soldiers killed her father. Her current whereabouts are unknown.

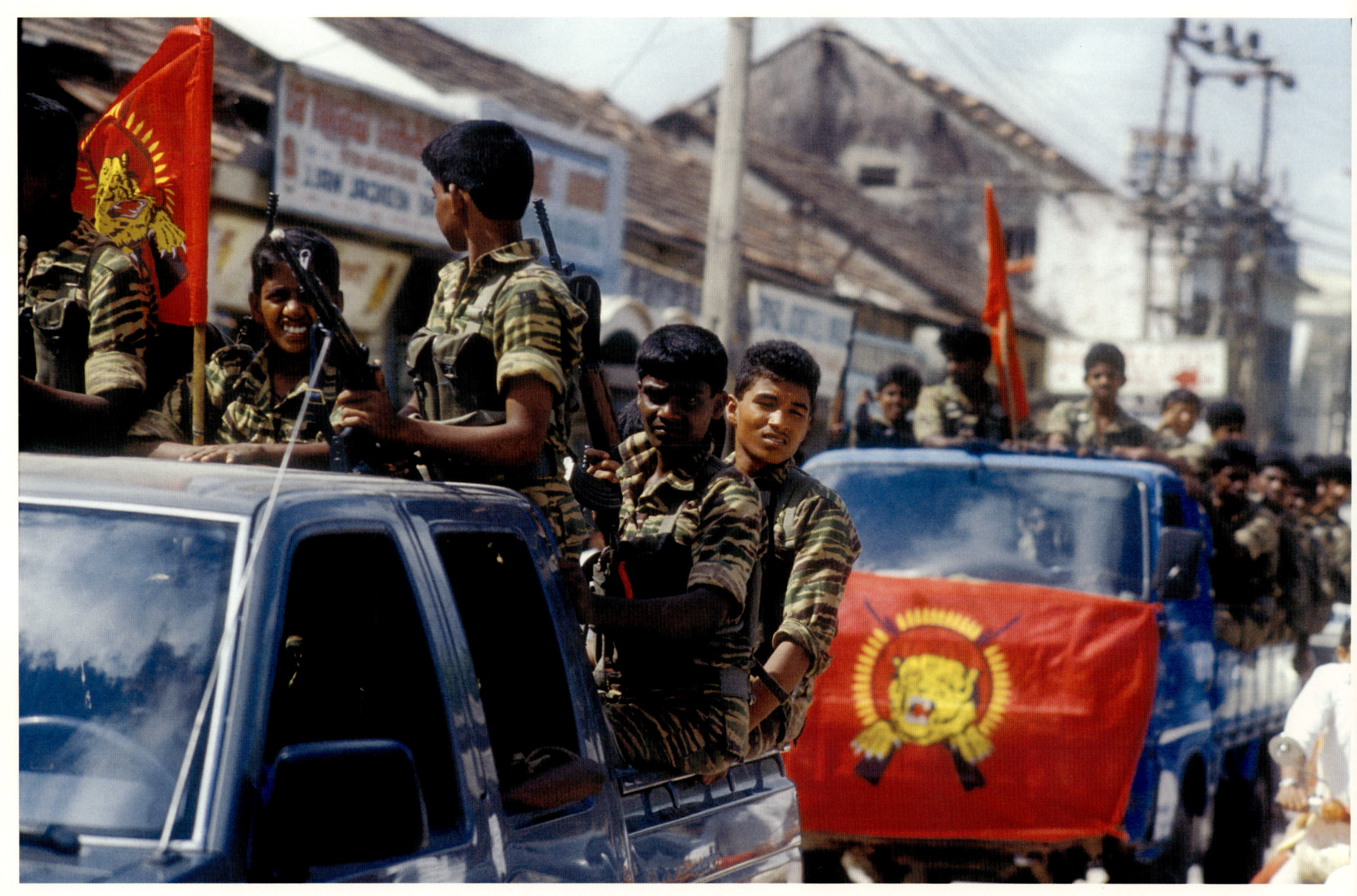

A Liberation Tigers of Tamil Eelam (LTTE) cadre of child soldiers rides through a Sri Lankan village. Photograph by Dominic Sansoni

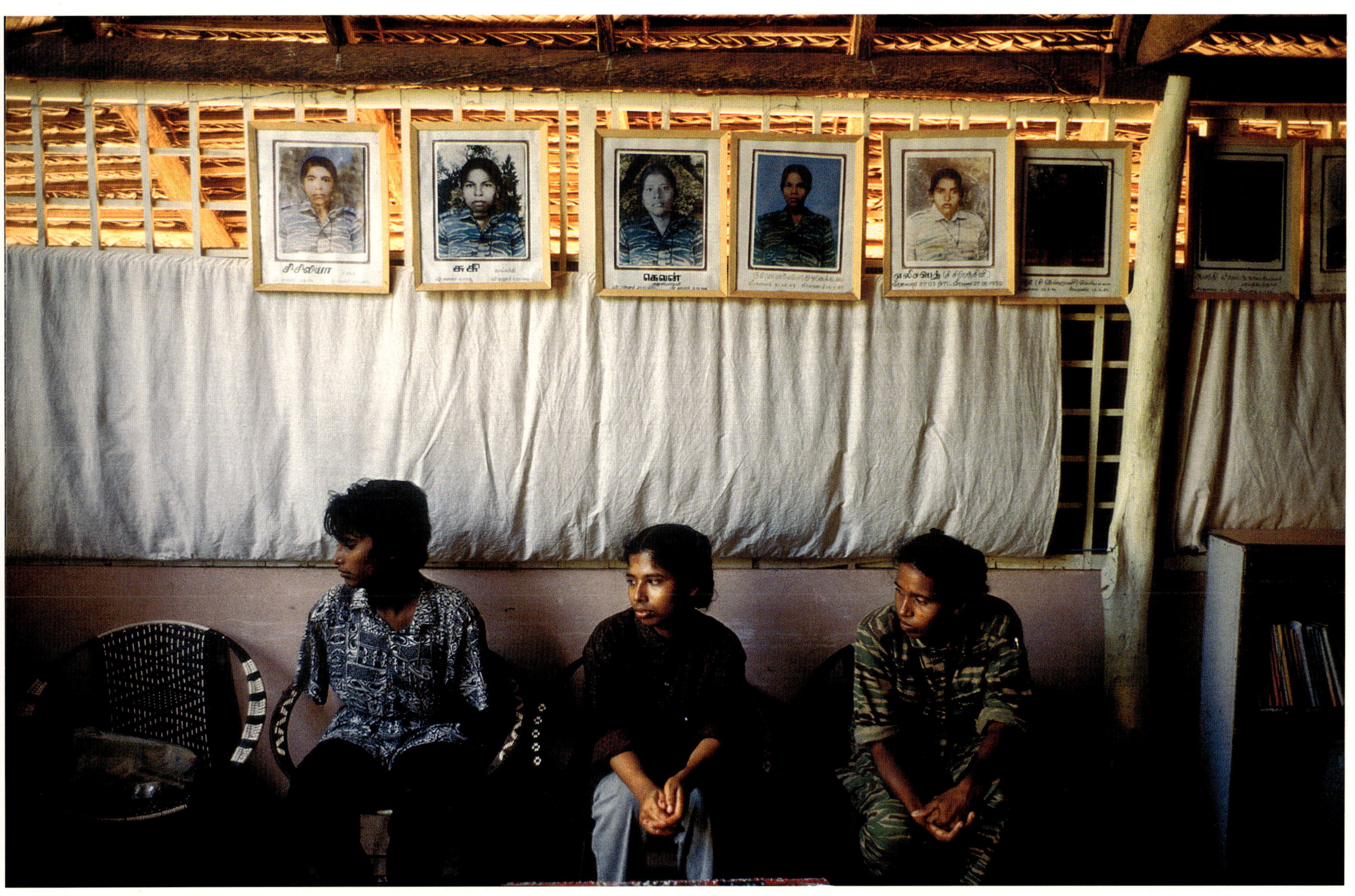

Three girl soldiers sit beneath pictures of killed comrades; one girl lost both arms in combat. Photograph by Dominic Sansoni

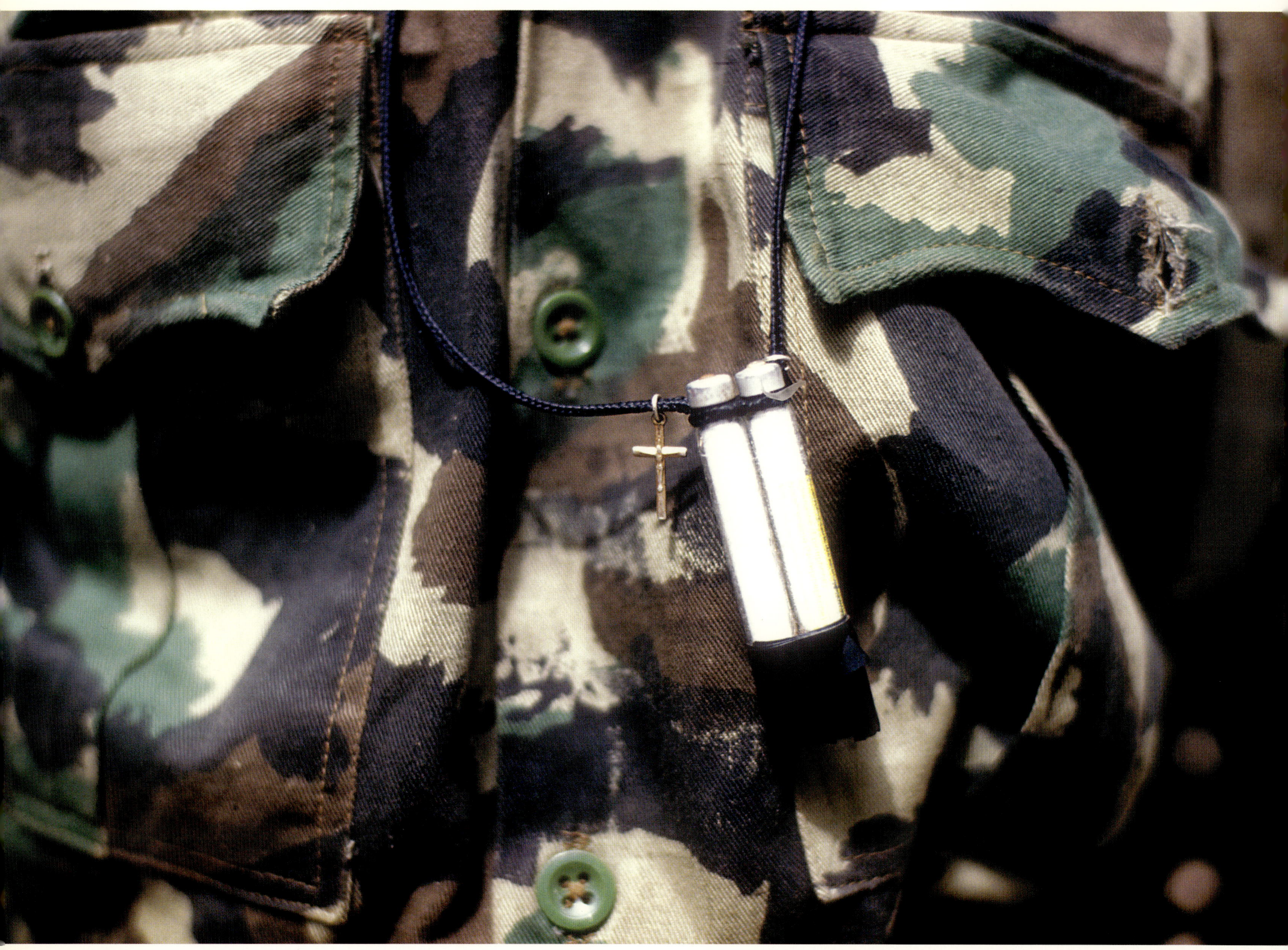

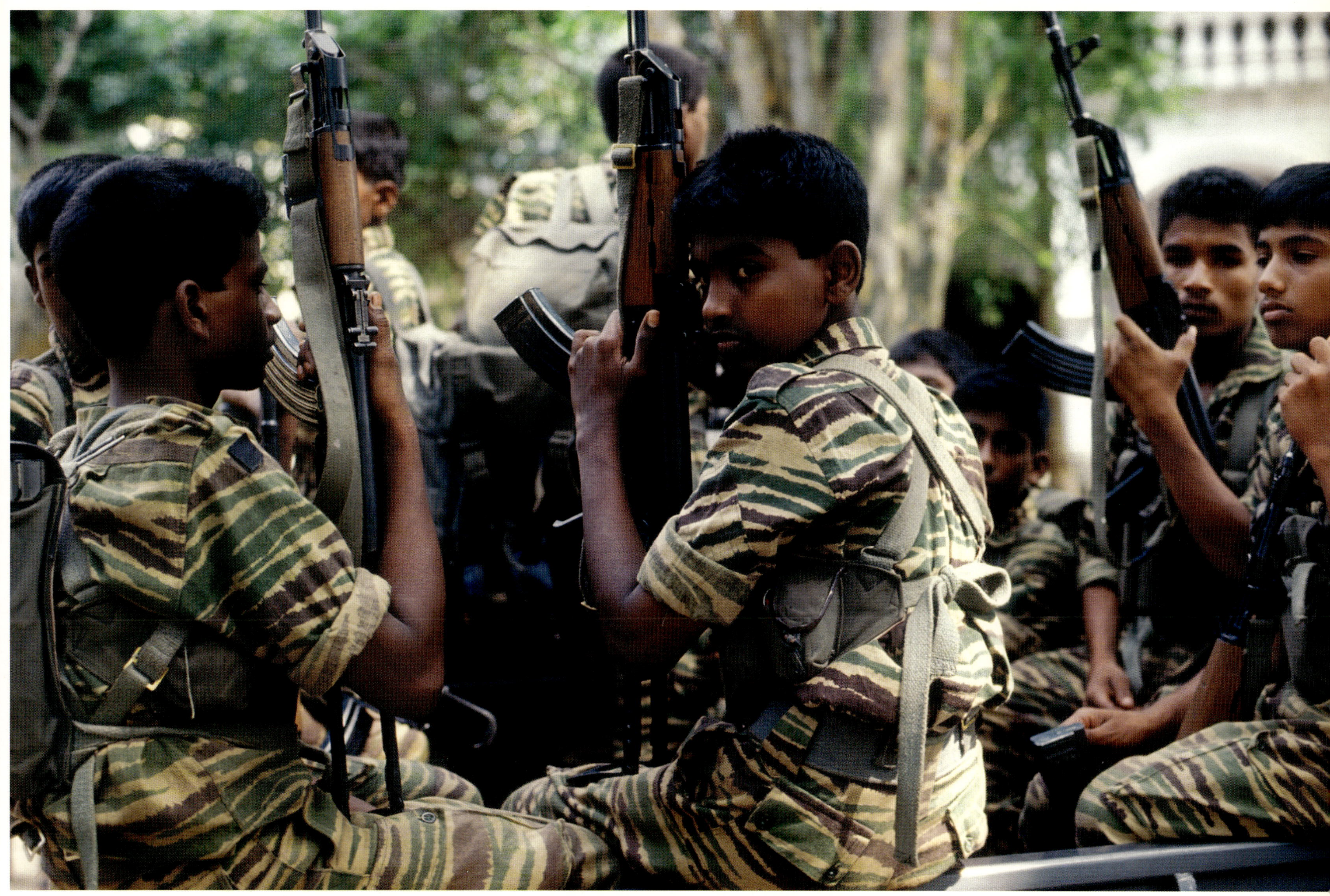

Left: Cyanide capsules worn around a young Tamil Tiger's neck. Above: A group of child Tamil Tigers sit in a truck on their way to battle. Photographs by Dominic Sansoni

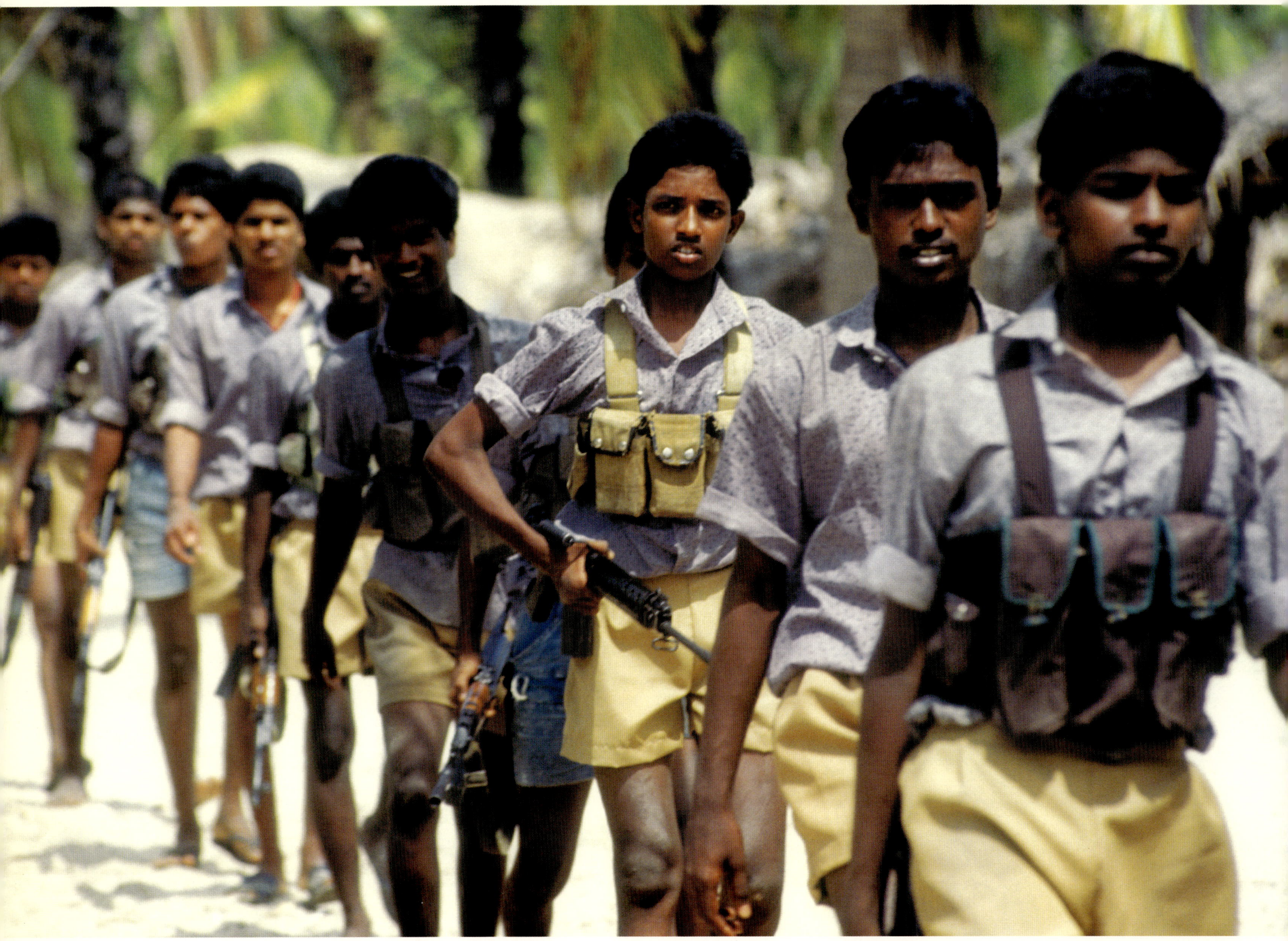

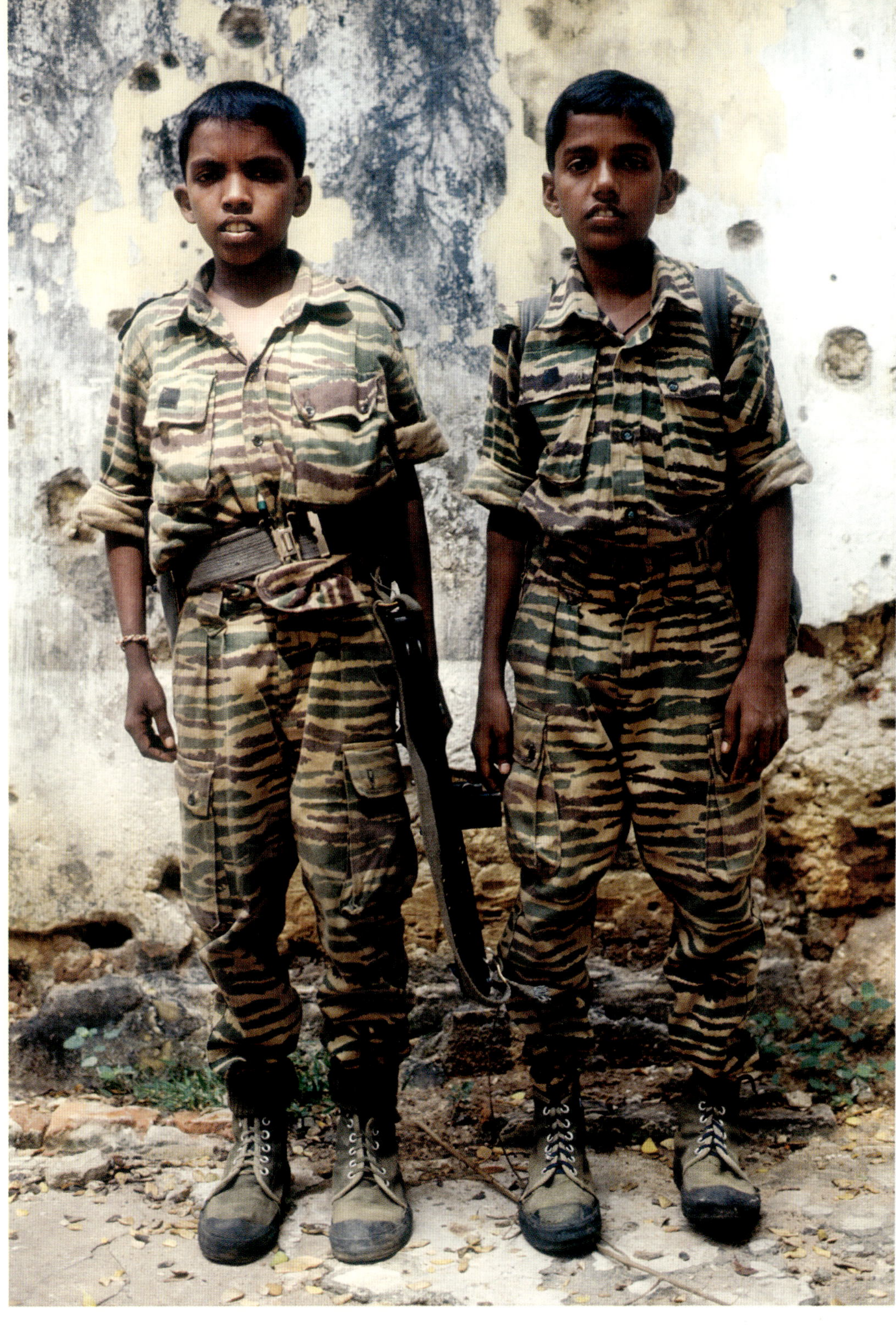

Left: A large LTTE training camp with training facilities on the Jaffna Peninsula. Above: Two young Tamil Tigers. Photographs by Dominic Sansoni

asia: burma

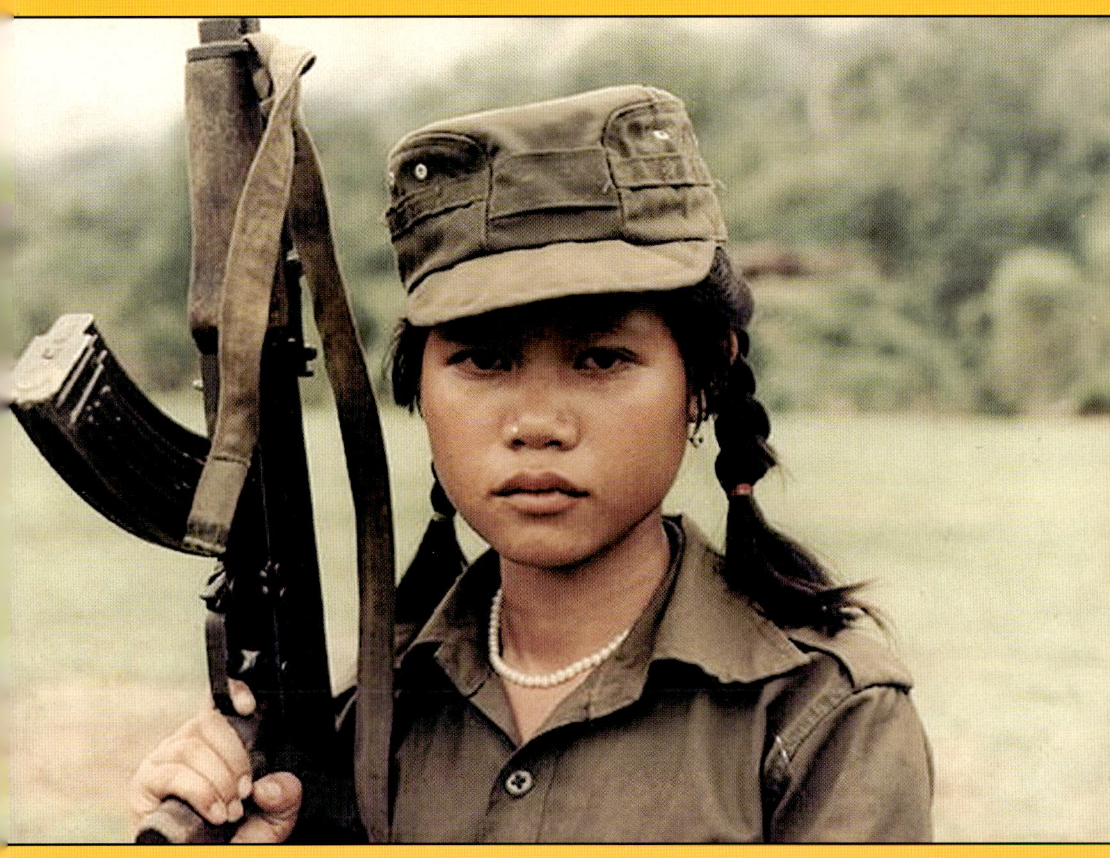

Nicky was raised in Kawthoolei, the province of the ethnic Karen in Burma.

At the age of 15, after witnessing the Burmese army burning her village, she decided to enlist in the Karen National Liberation Army.

At the time she enlisted, women were not allowed to train alongside the men. A special unit of soldiers was set up to facilitate the induction of young women into the ranks of the guerilla resistance.

Though the women retain separate living quarters and train separately, they fight alongside their male counterparts. Nicky's parents supported her decision to become a soldier. Like all Karen who live in Burma, they wish for a democratic society and live in fear of a military junta. Their war has gone on for over 50 years and is now a way of life.

Photograph by Peter Mantello

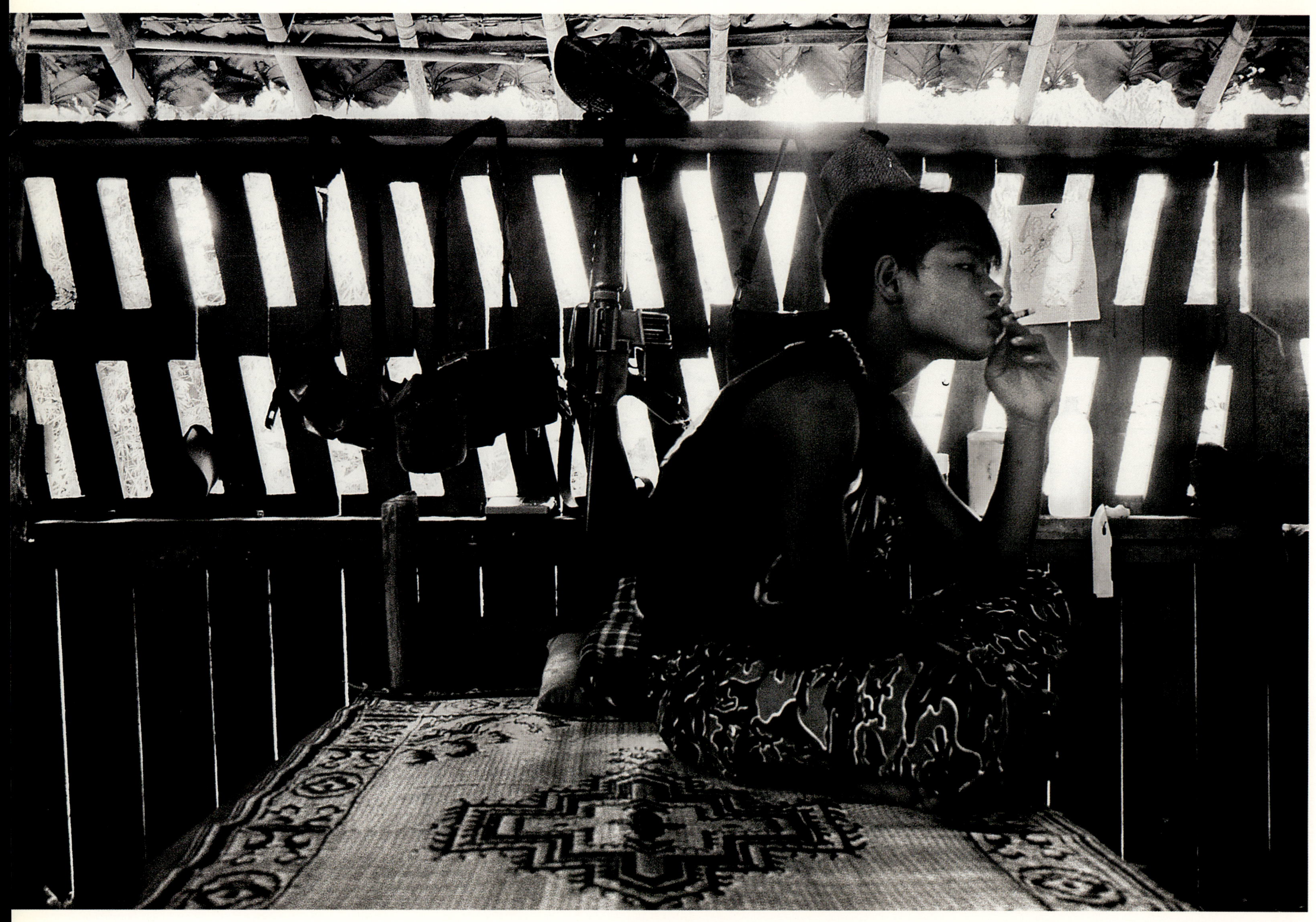

Above: A 17-year-old commander of the KNLA has been fighting since he was 12 years old. Membership passes from father to son. Photograph by Alvaro Ybarra Zavala/Agence VU. Left: A young soldier rests with his weapon. Photograph by Peter Mantello

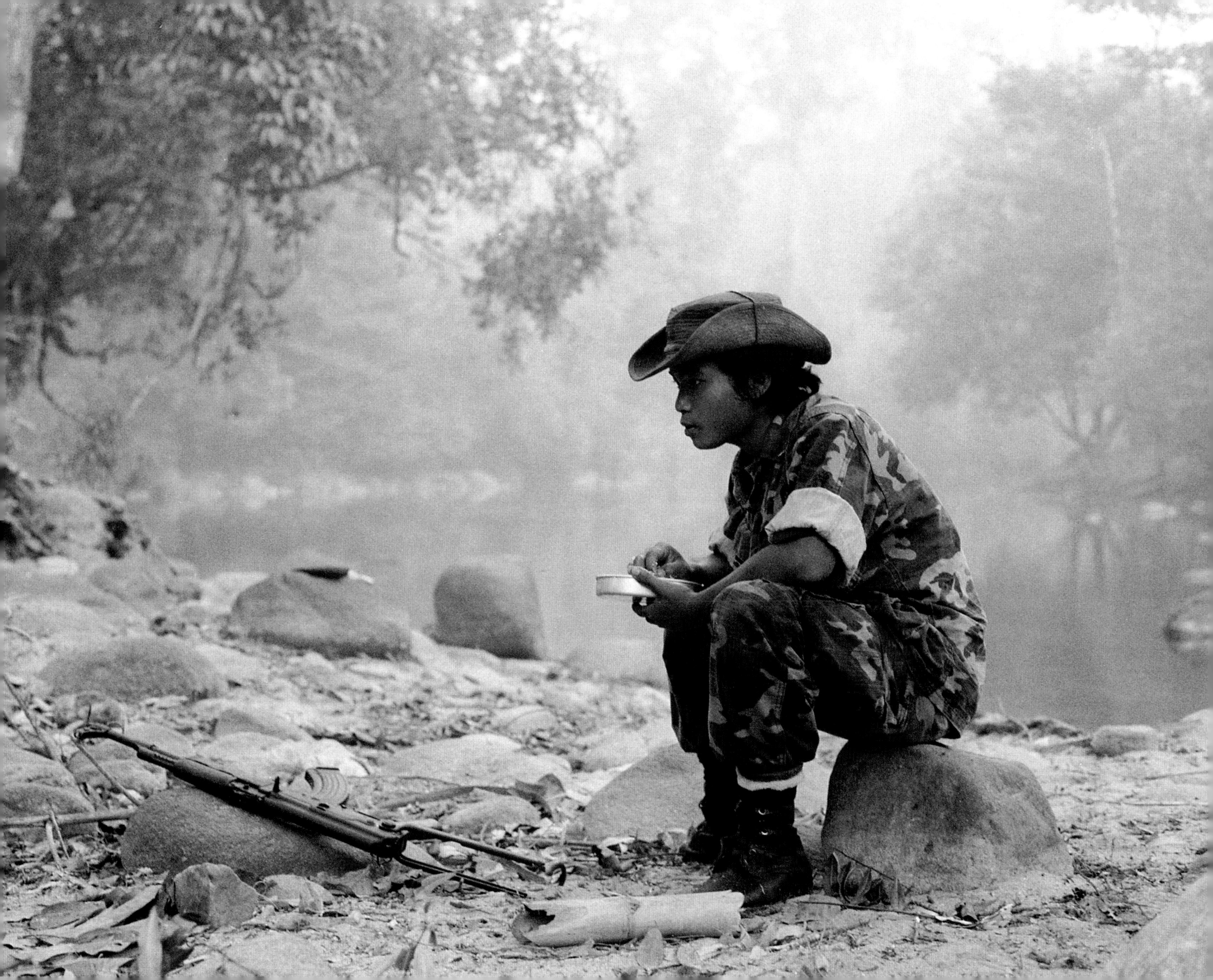

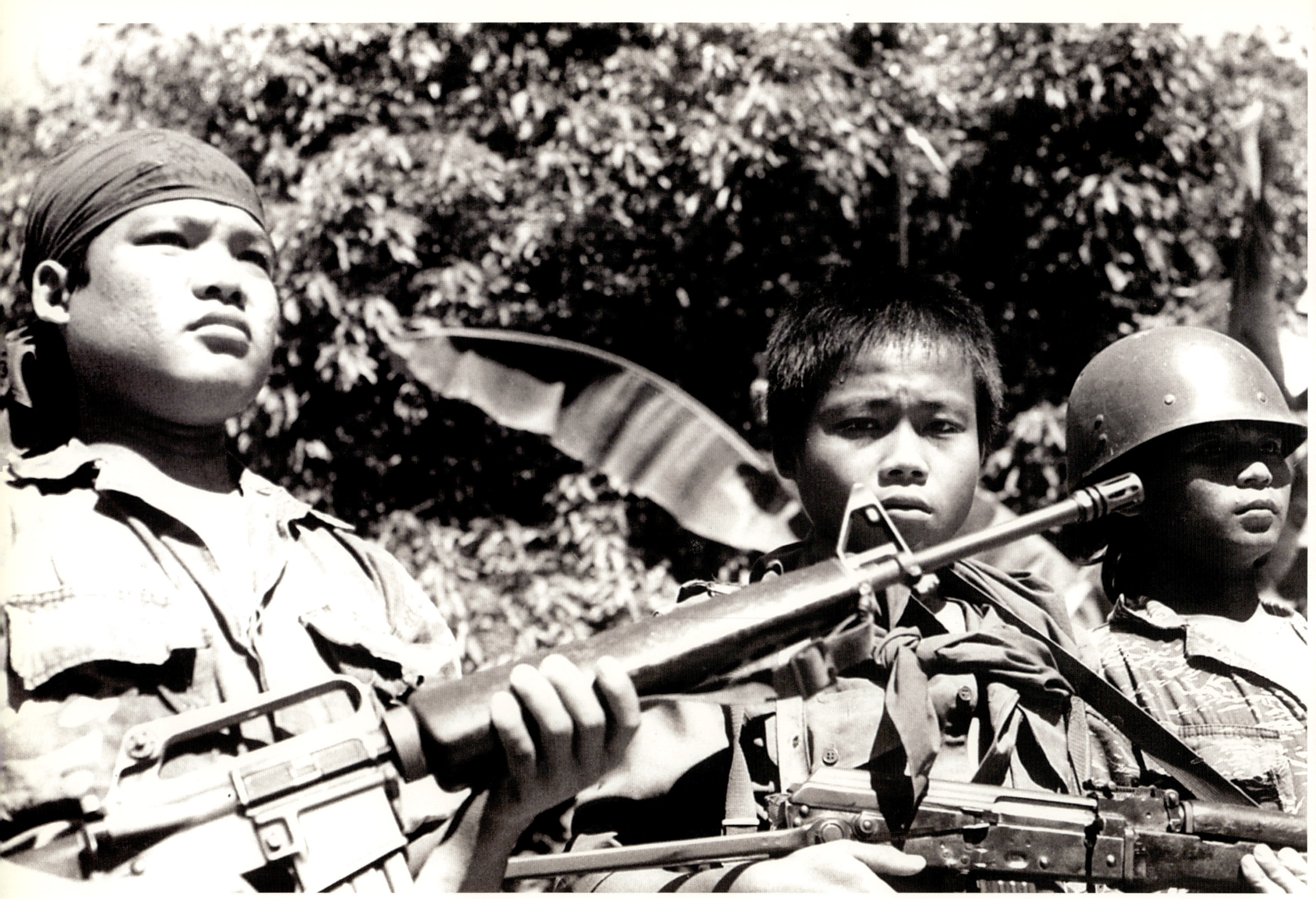

Above: Along the Thai-Burmese border, small groups of child soldiers protect their village strongholds with unflinching conviction and determination. Right: A newly enlisted Karen boy stands at attention in the light of early morning at Karen National Army Headquarters. Photographs by Peter Mantello

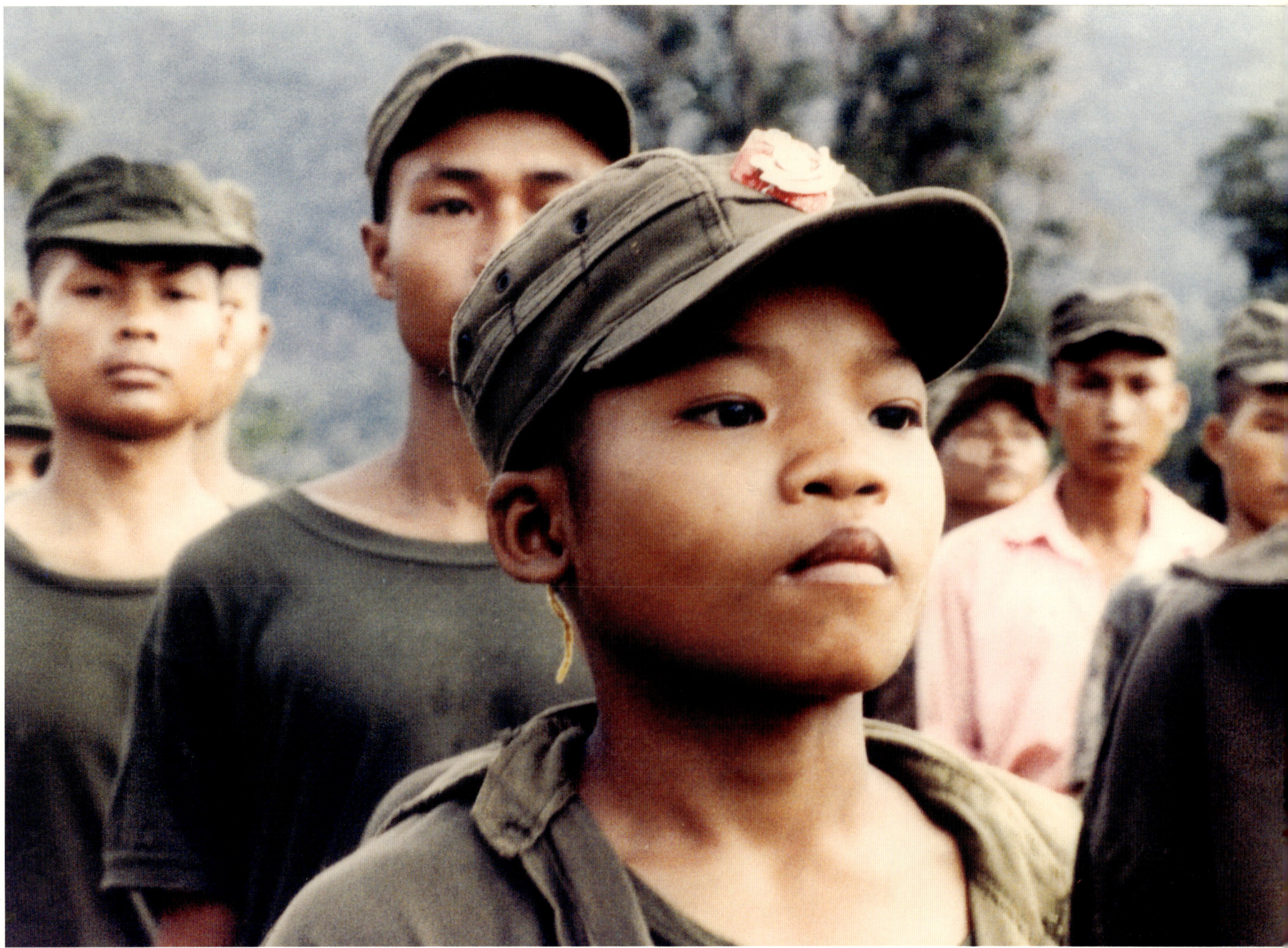

asia: nepal

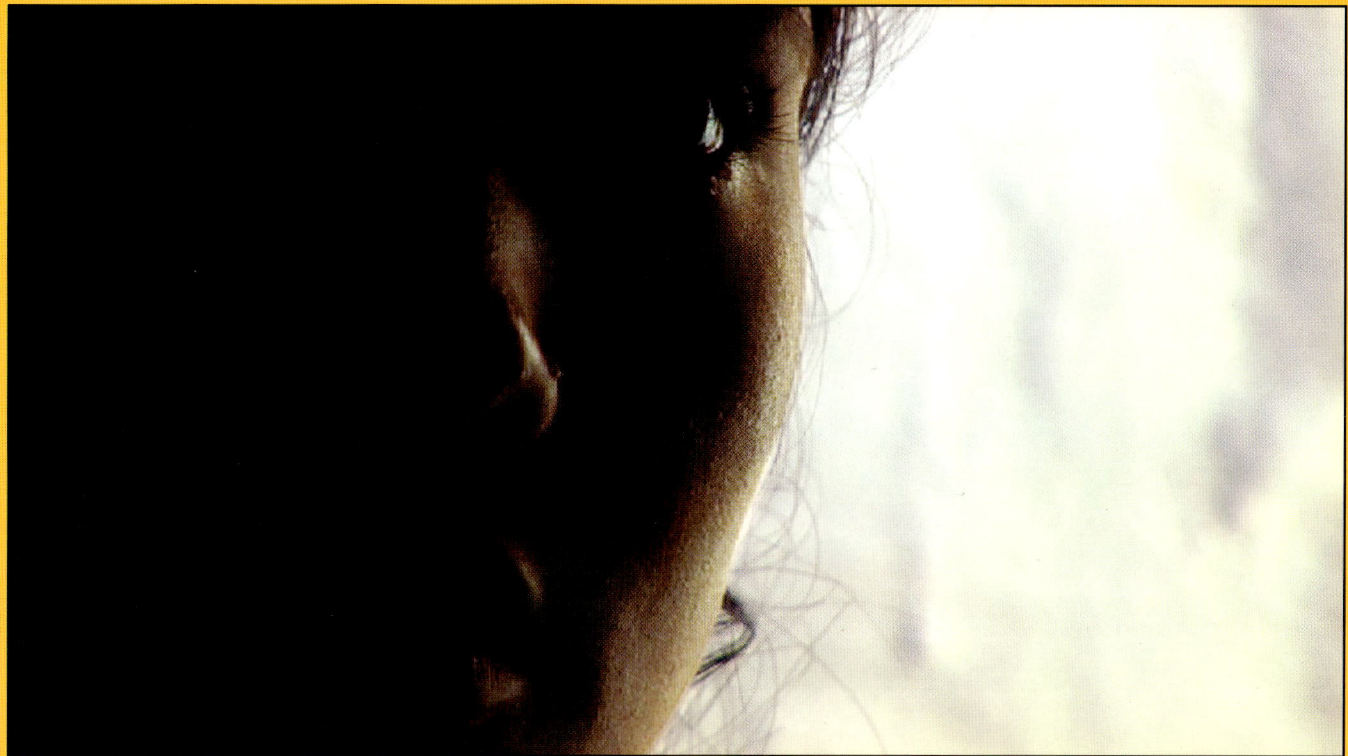

Photograph by Bob Koenig

"My name is Asha. I have my parents, brothers, and sisters at home. I was 14 when I got involved in the [Maoist] party. I am now 17 years old.

I quit school because I had to do household work and look after my younger siblings. The didis* would come regularly. Other didis would also come and tell me to attend their programs. When I went to listen to the program, I didn't feel like coming back. Then I worked for the party. I visited my house once after joining. I came back with the sisters, and my parents scolded me and told me not to go there again. Then, I didn't feel like staying at home.

I did various duties like carrying and sending letters and walking with the sisters. I distributed letters, glued party posters on walls, carried the pillars of the entry gates from place to place, and helped to organize programs.

I once saw an incident in a nearby district. All the party workers were involved in a cultural program. While the program was taking place, the army surrounded the hall downstairs with guns drawn. We were scared. The brothers of the party told us to get out of there and said that they would handle the situation. We escaped and I don't know what happened to them afterwards.

I worry about my present situation because of my affiliation with Maoists. I have nightmares. I feel as if somebody is threatening to kill me. I feel as if somebody is scolding me harshly and threatening me, so I get petrified from time to time."

* "Didi" literally means older sisters, but is used as a respectful term to describe an older non-related girl and/or woman.

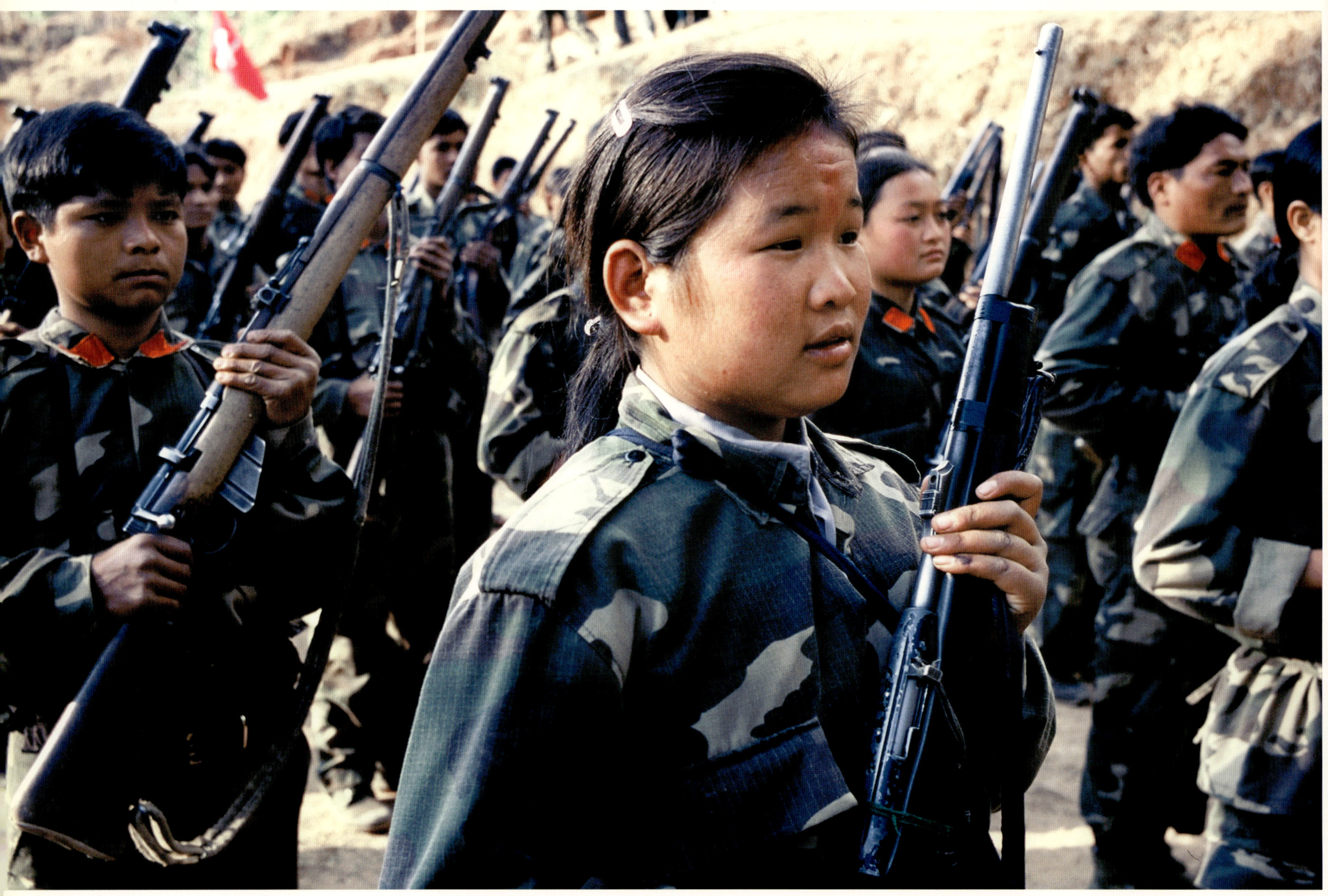

Maoist rebel soldiers stand in line during a drill. Photograph by Tomas van Houtryve/Panos

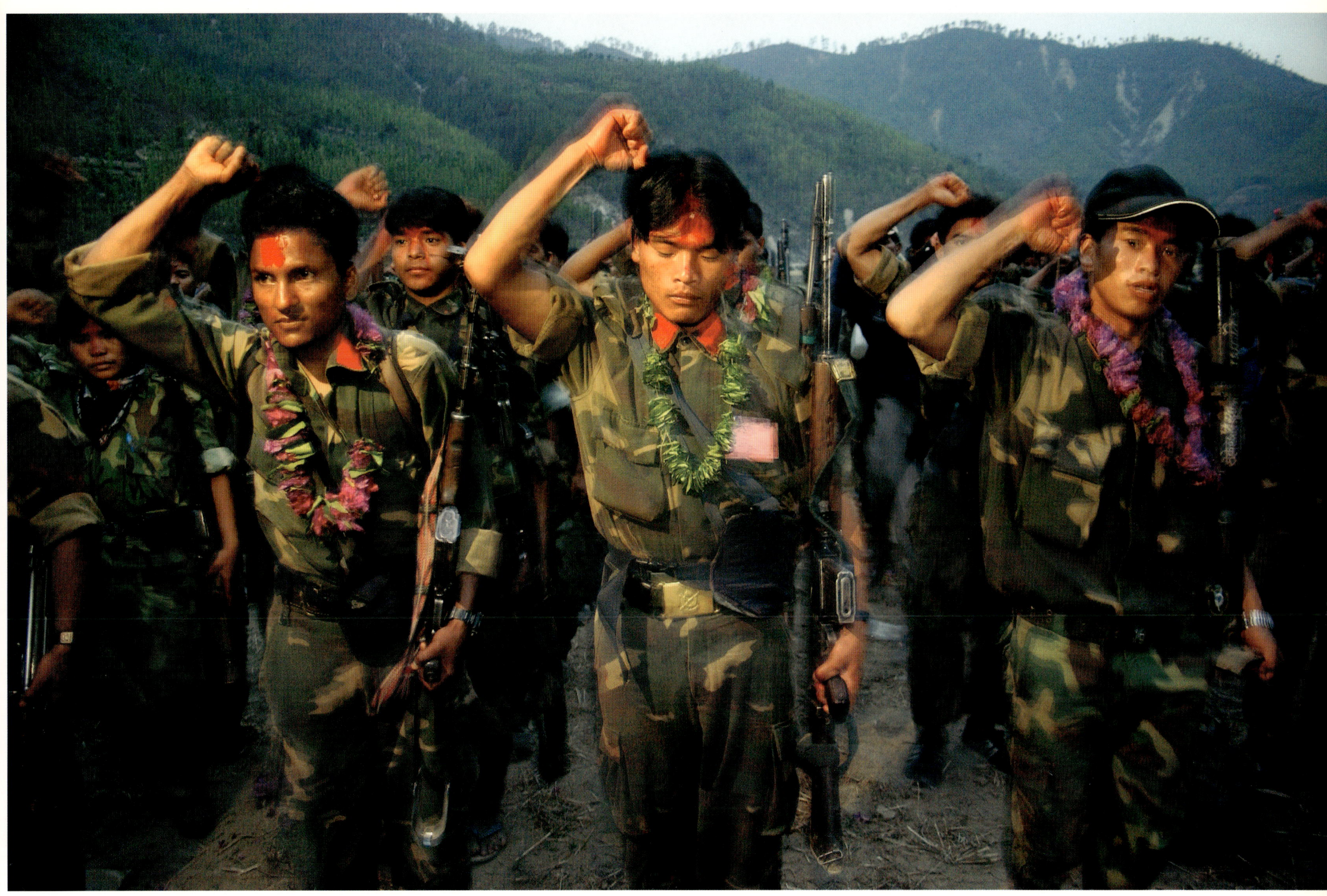

Maoist insurgents, many of them children, celebrate in the Rukum district, weeks after their attack on government troops in Beni. Photograph by Ami Vitale

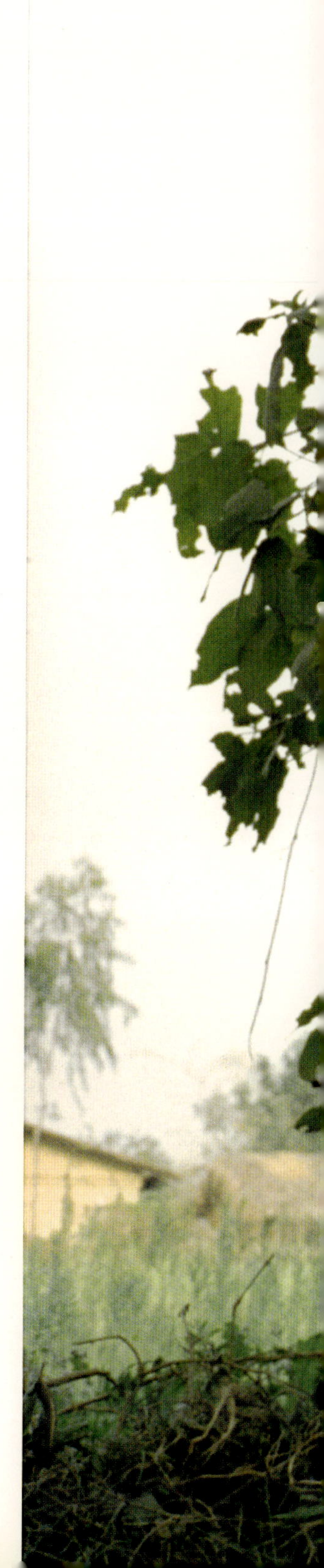

A teenager stands guard outside a village controlled by Maoist rebels in Nepal. Photograph by Tiane Doan na Champassak/Agence VU

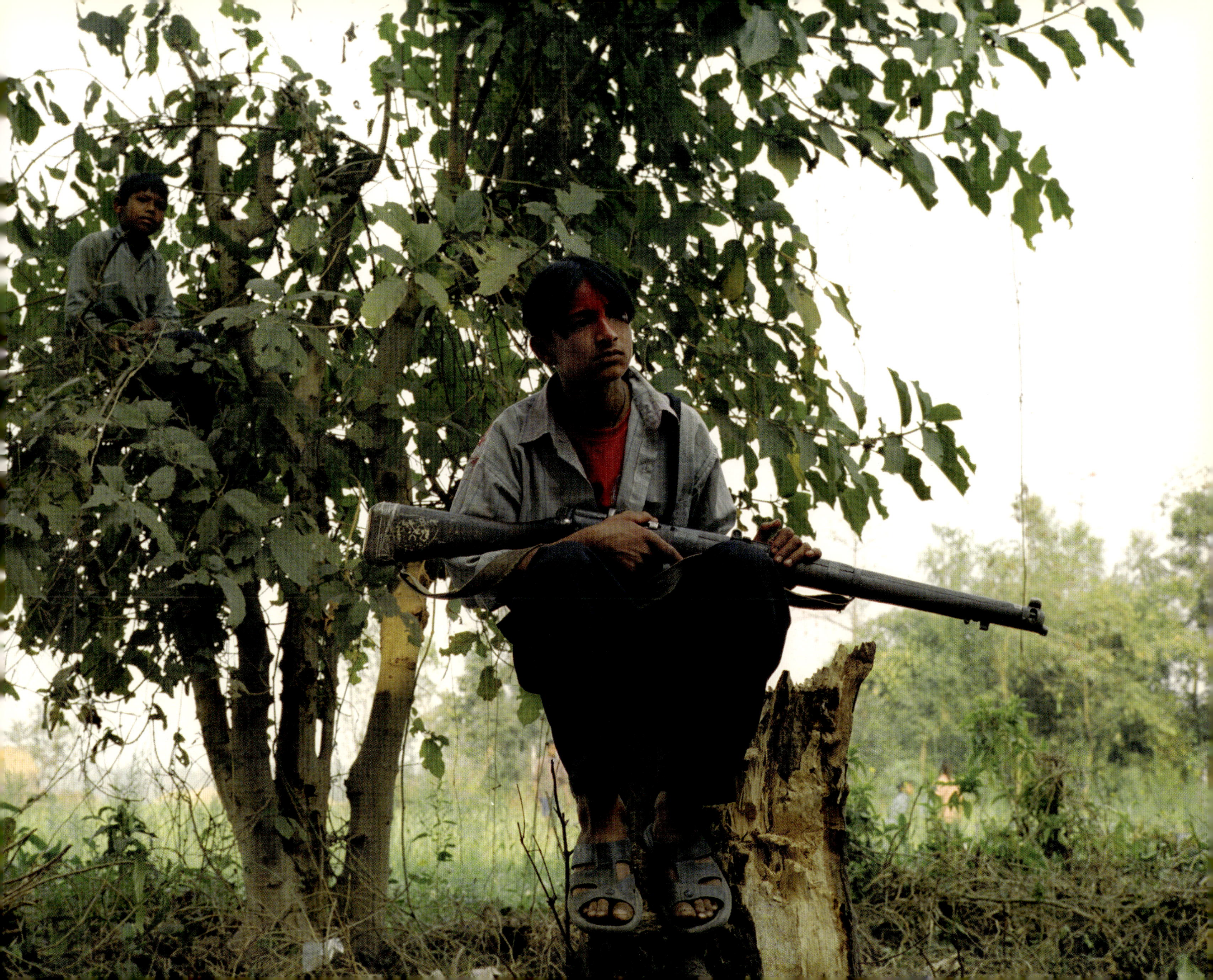

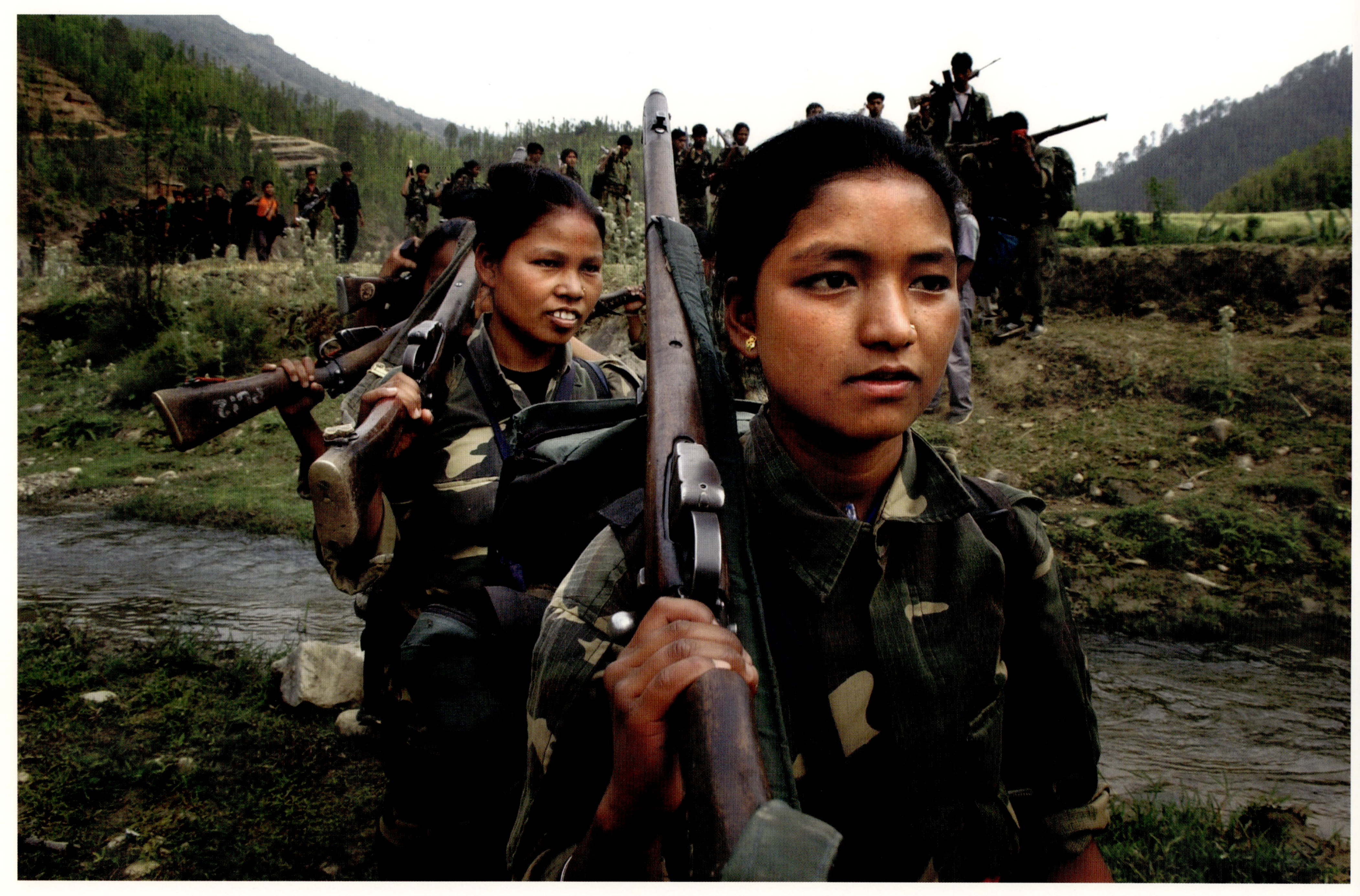

The Maoist rebels return from the Beni district government headquarters where they looted a bank, destroyed the jail, and torched government office buildings. Photograph by Ami Vitale

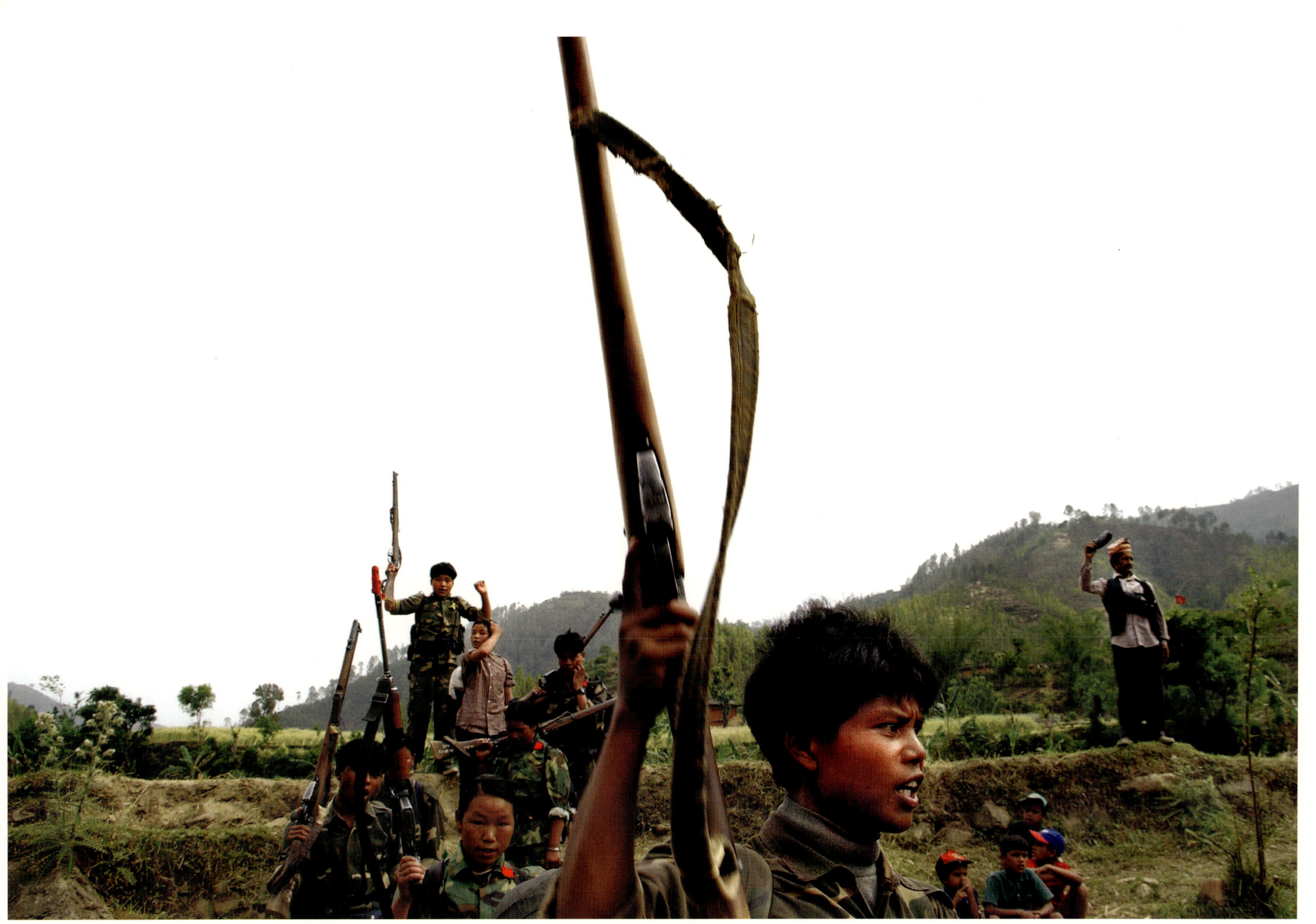

Maoist insurgents, including many children, celebrate a victory in the Rukum district. Photograph by Ami Vitale

a: afghanistan

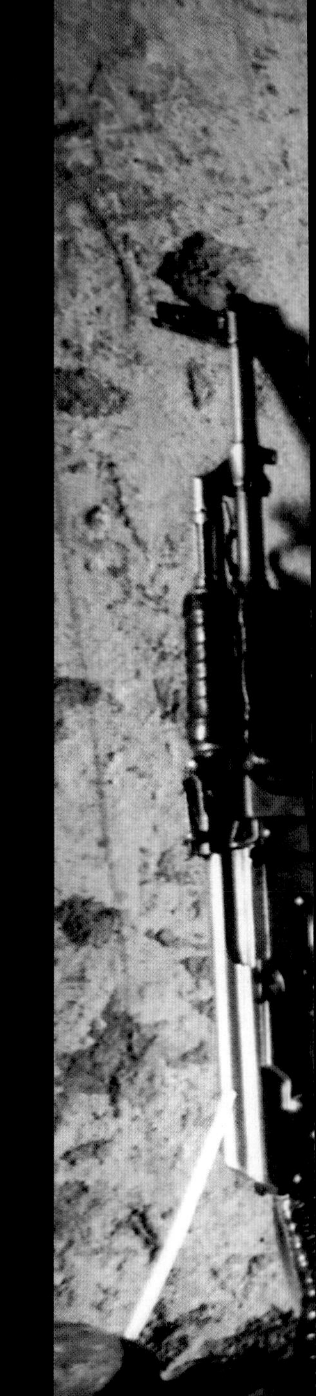

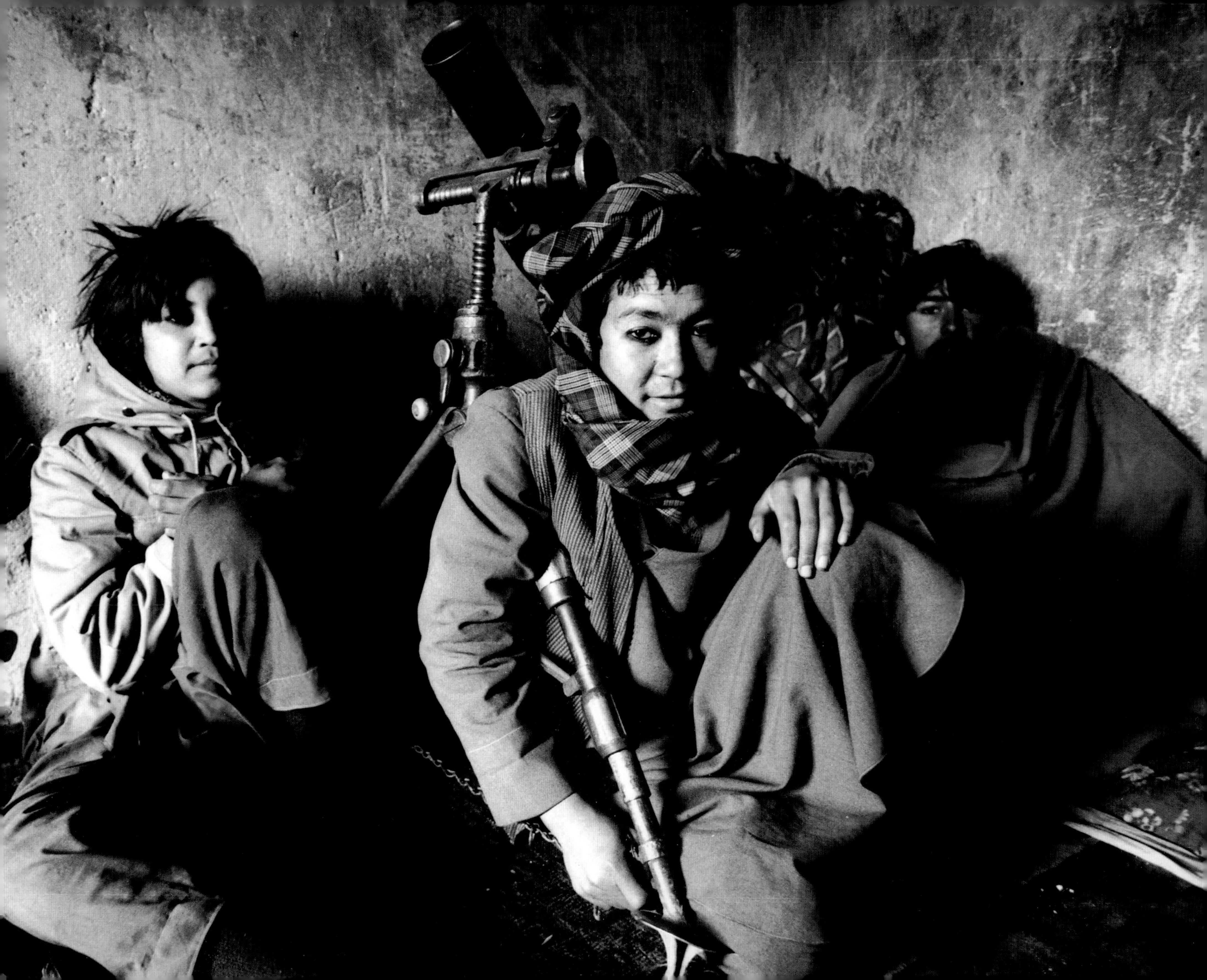

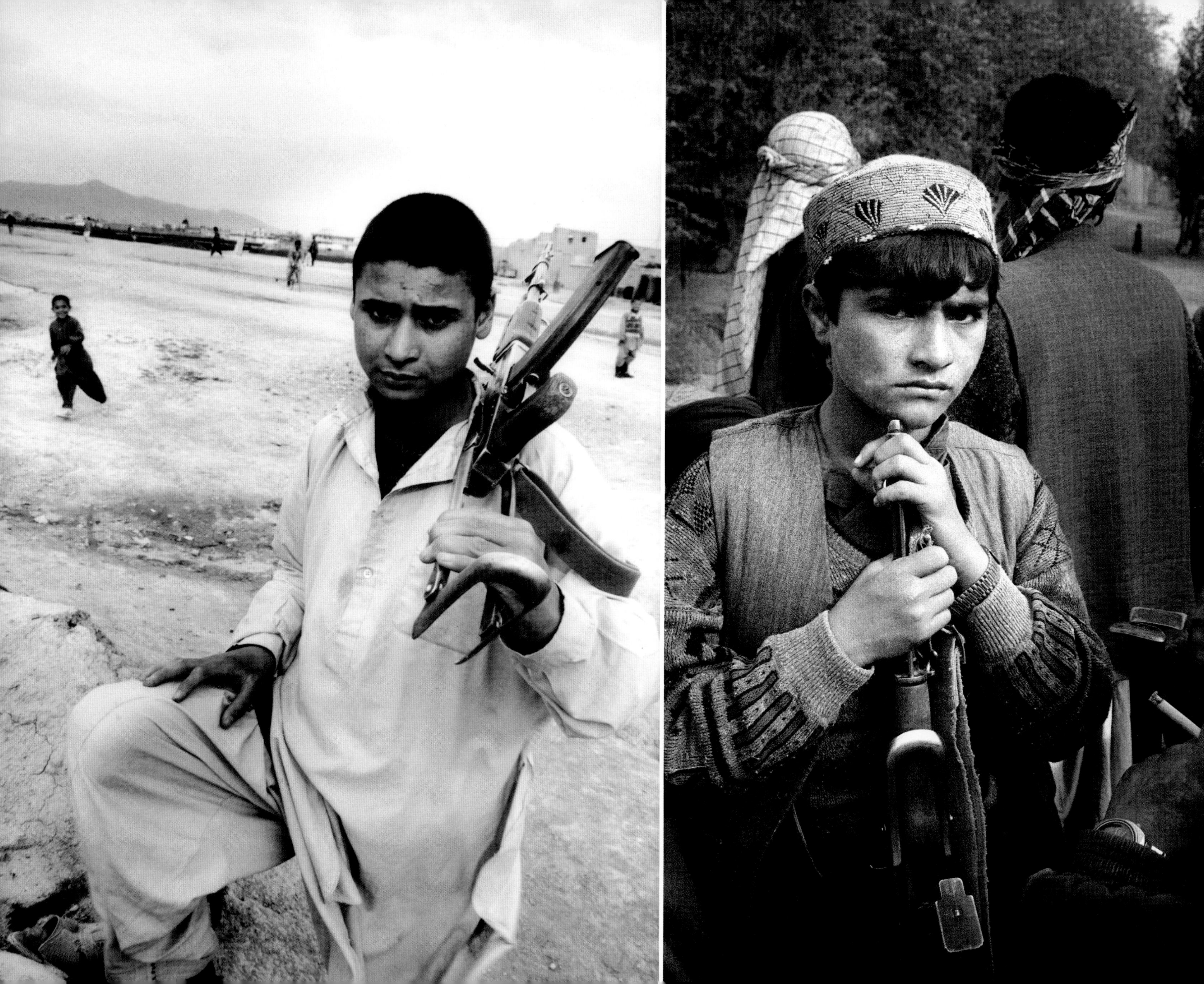

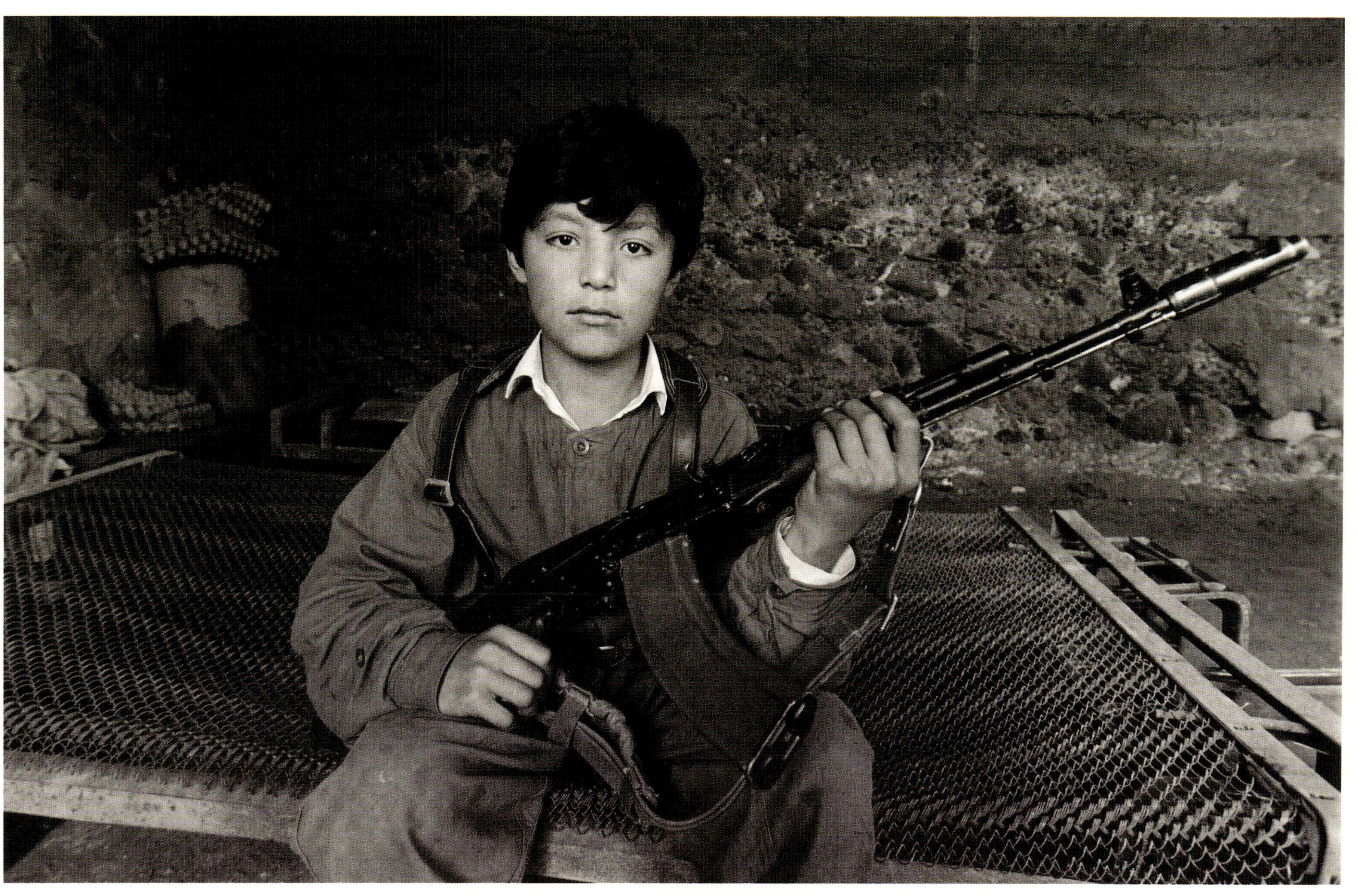

Far left: A 15-year-old Afghan soldier in Kabul. Photograph by Q. Sakamaki. Left: A young boy fighting for the Northern Alliance sits on the back of a truck heading for the frontline. Photograph by Francesco Zizola/Noor. Above: A 14-year-old boy who fights on the Azeri/Armenian border. Photograph by Zed Nelson/Panos

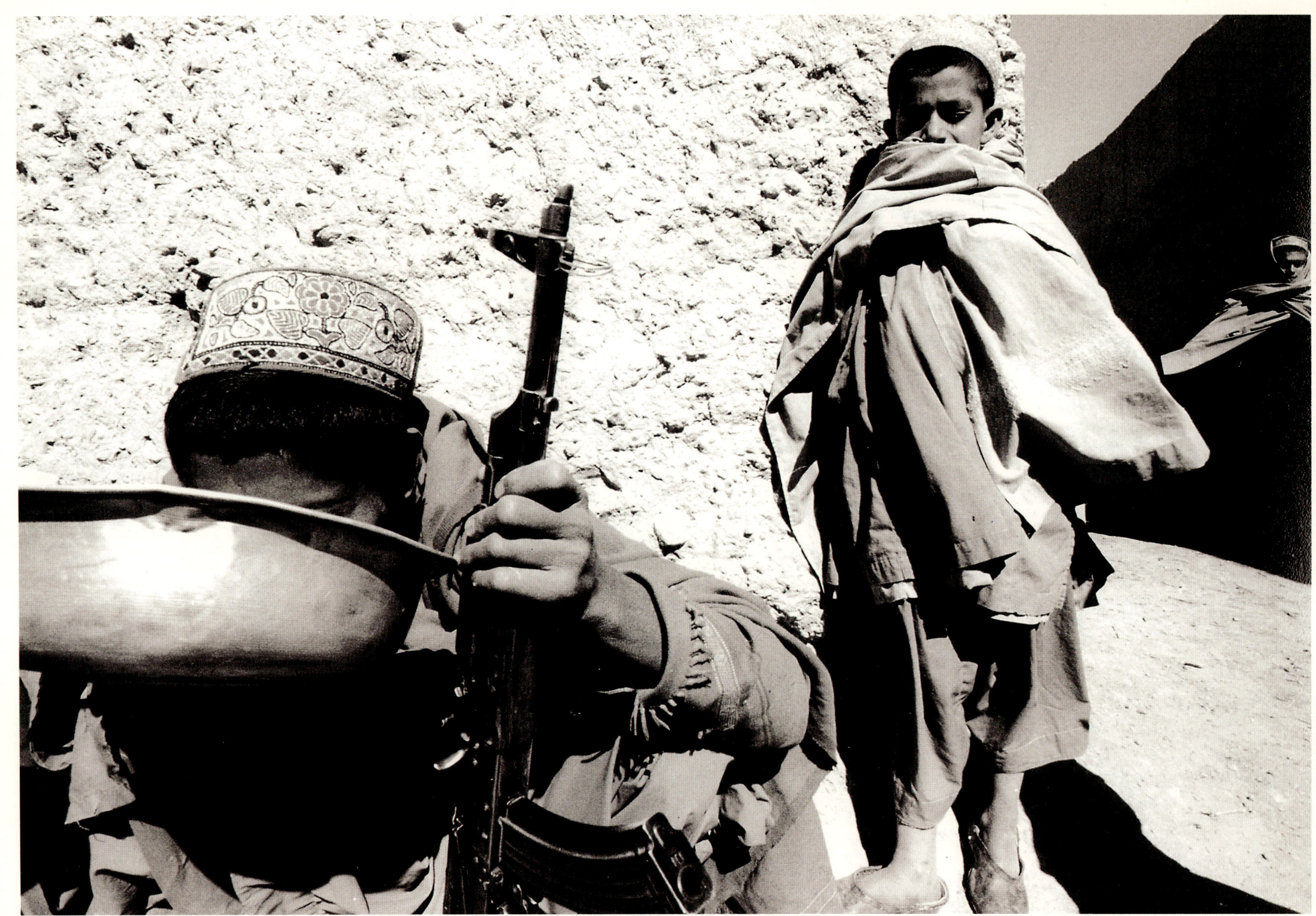

Two boys holding weapons stop to drink. Photograph by Francesco Cito/Panos

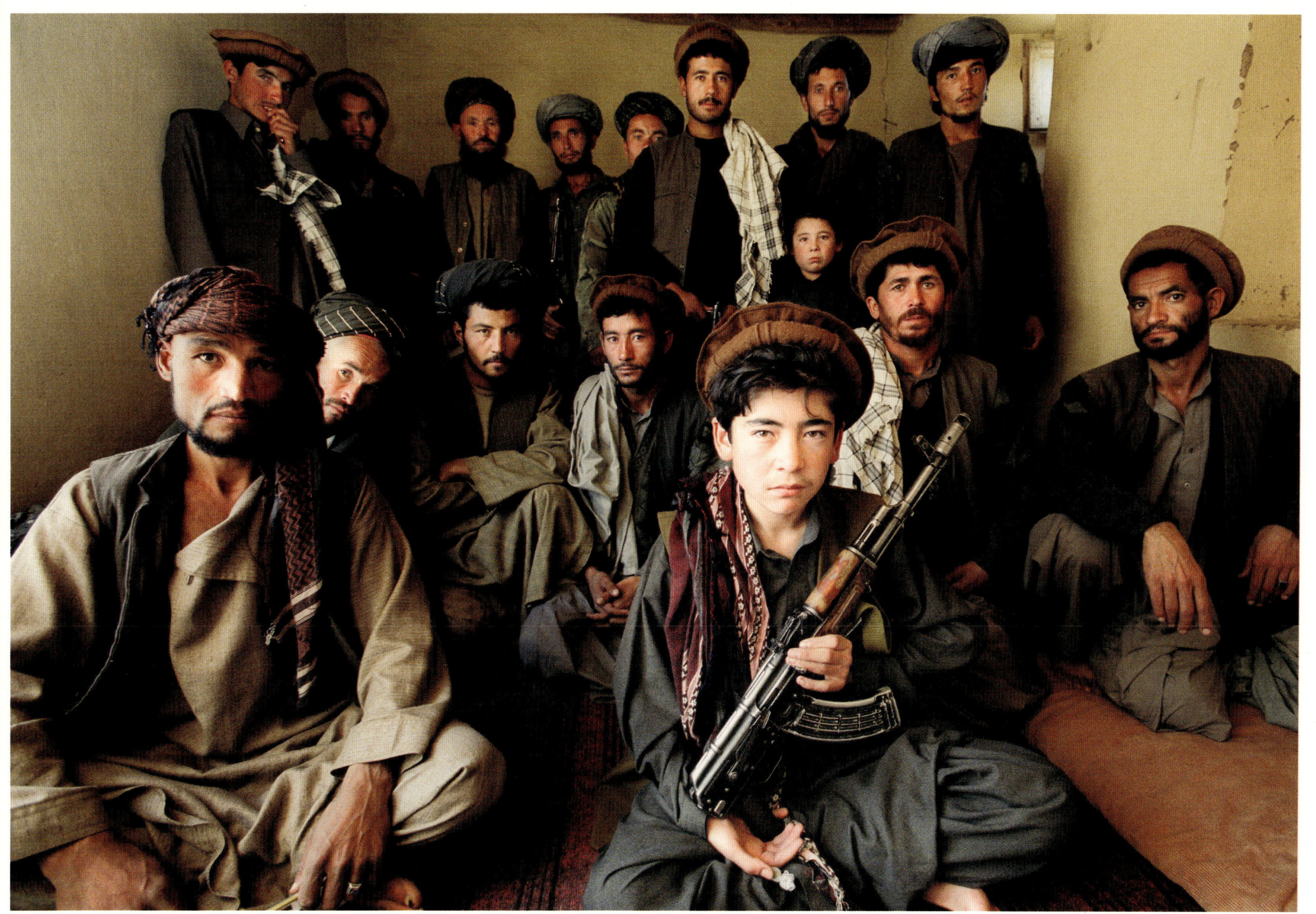

A teenage Northern Alliance warlord in Haq Bullaq, surrounded by bodyguards and soldiers. Photograph by Martin Adler/Panos

A Cry for Help in a Forest Far Away

Jimmie Briggs

On a Saturday afternoon several years ago, I picked up the newspaper to find an all-too-familiar face staring back at me. In a front-page color picture, a Liberian gunman knelt in a city street, howling in anger while pointing an automatic rifle at the photographer who had captured his image. More chilling than the weapon he held was what he wore on his back: a pink teddy-bear backpack, a telling symbol of his lost youth.

In a number of African nations, children have been used as foot soldiers to fight on behalf of adult commanders. Ten years ago, I had my first encounter with child soldiers in Zaire—now the Democratic Republic of Congo—while covering the fall of the late dictator Mobutu Sese Seko. I stared at the preteen boys holding rifles taller than themselves. Some had relatively mundane duties—as guards, carrying their commanders' bags, or doing kitchen work. Most, however, saw frontline combat, erasing all but the bare vestiges of their childhoods with each round fired from their AK-47s. With their too-large uniforms, slight builds, and smooth faces, they could have been youngsters playing a game of war. But the vacant look in their eyes was that of old soldiers.

In the years since, I've traveled the world talking with young African, Latin, Asian, and Middle Eastern boys and girls engaged in battle, as well as those lucky enough to have survived their experiences and escaped.

I remember one 16-year-old boy named François who lived in Gitarama during the genocide, whom I met in the lush green hills of Rwanda. He was also a victim, but in a very different way. The son of a Tutsi mother and Hutu father, he was abducted from his rural hillside home by a Hutu mob, along with his grandmother, mother, sisters, and nieces and nephews. On May 11, 1994, the mob led François and his family to the edge of a mass grave. One of his sisters, who intended to marry a Tutsi, was killed immediately and dumped into the grave. Then they presented a Solomonic choice to his mother: "Give us 5,000 francs and we kill your daughter's children; otherwise your son will do it for us," they told her. "My son is not a killer," she shot back. "Then we will teach him," was their cold reply. Scared and unsure of what to do, François says he stood at the edge of the ravine that contained his sister's and other bodies. One of the men started beating him with a stick. At that point, he says, he realized he might die. Reluctantly, François picked up a hoe and crushed the skulls of his young nieces and nephews. He remembers their eyes staring up at him in disbelief as he beat the life out of them. When he was finished, their limp bodies were pushed into the grave. After François returned home, his family told him: "You had no choice, but it was a horrible thing."

Some would argue that America faces its own version of this problem with gun-carrying child "fighters," members of gangs and drug rings. The trauma American youth face through urban violence is similar to conflict and post-conflict situations. But the degree of devastation is quite different. In countries abroad where children have taken up arms, voluntarily or by force, there has been a breakdown in society, making the youngsters even more vulnerable to war's abuses.

"From now on, you're our soldier," the rebels told Oyet Lamony. "If you try to escape, you will be killed. If you talk to a girl, you will be killed." These were the two rules of survival that guided Lamony, who is now 17. Five years ago, he was kidnapped from his village of Kitgum, in northern Uganda. When the rebels entered his village, they asked for all the young males. The local people replied that there were none—except for Lamony. Caught unaware at home, he was taken into the bush with other abducted area youths.

"I stayed with them quite a long time," Lamony told me shortly after his escape, at a rehabilitation center in the town of Gulu. "They made us overpower a group of government soldiers and take their weapons. Then we had to cut them up with pangas [machetes]. The rebels told me that if I refused, they would kill me. Another boy was chopped up as an example. So, I killed the three government soldiers."

The rebels marched Lamony to a camp in southern Sudan. There, he was wounded twice in battles with Dinka tribesmen. It took him three years to carry out his escape. When Lamony and I met, he was receiving counseling and medical treatment at a Gulu trauma center that specialized in helping children who had had similar experiences.

The more I travel, the more I'm reminded that most of the horrible, tragic acts perpetrated by human beings are directed at children—or committed by them. I know this from having spent time with girl soldiers in Colombia who have fled their military commanders for fear of having their unborn babies destroyed—being pregnant isn't synonymous with being a good soldier. (Most of them had been impregnated by fellow soldiers.) These "lost girls" are a hidden part of the violence puzzle, are rarely exposed as much as their male counterparts.

There was hope in Afghanistan. Shortly after the United States invaded and overthrew the Taliban, in the heady rush of a post-9/11 world, I met courageous young people including girls and women who threw off their hijabs, strolled in public with men who were not husbands or relatives, went to university, and participated in the reconstruction of their country. Abbreviated freedom has a bitter taste; today, these same women are covered head-to-toe, faceless, without identities. The most desperate try to escape by setting themselves on fire; others remain and risk honor killings or acid attacks.

These experiences must be recognized, must be honored. On one of my first trips to northern Uganda, an elderly man told me that if a dying person tells you their story, and it's not passed on, you'll be haunted. Well, I do pass on every story I hear, but the knowledge, the awareness, remains to haunt me.

François Minani, the half-Tutsi, half-Hutu young man I met in Rwanda, was tried on September 23, 1997 for taking part in the genocide. He pleaded guilty and asked the court for forgiveness. Eventually, he was served three years at Gitarama Central Prison. François says prayer and constant reflection helped him through the experience, but he returned home guilty and scarred. François lives in with a surviving sister and her children, as well as his wife and son. "I have forgiven myself for what happened, for what I did," he told me during the 10th anniversary of the genocide. It was a rainy April afternoon, and François was surrounded by his extended family and a few neighbors. Sitting in front of their modest, mud-brick home, François held his two-year-old son in his lap. "Sometimes when I think about it, I feel guilty, but at other times I don't. Always I ask myself, 'Why did the genocide happen?' I used to have nightmares, but now they have stopped," he admitted. "If I could go back to the day before the Hutus came, my life might be different. I was a very young boy and when you're a boy, sometimes you don't know what to do, what to choose."

Jimmie Briggs is a journalist and the author of Innocents Lost: When Child Soldiers Go to War *(Basic Books, 2005).*

africa: uganda

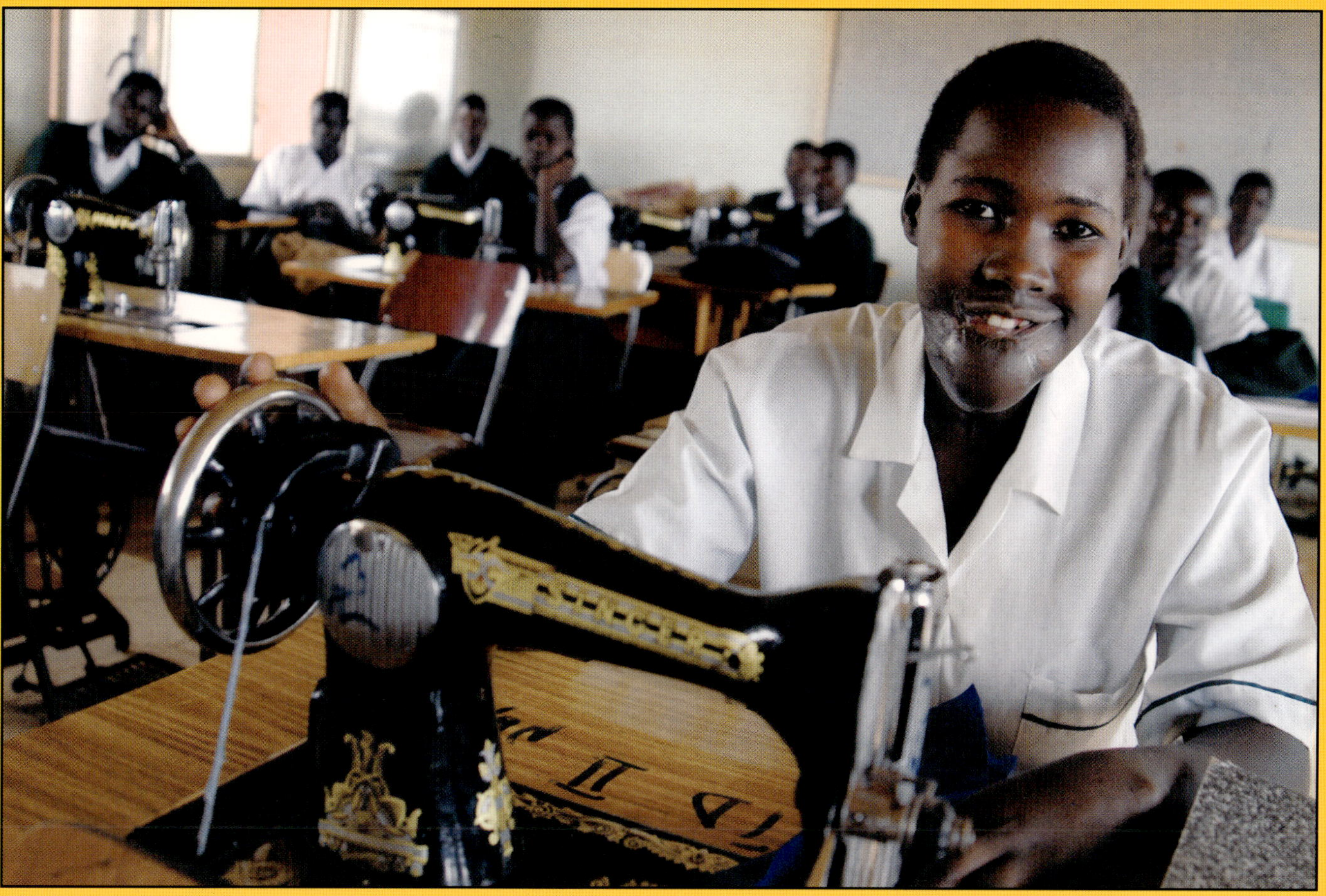

Photograph by Riccardo Gangale

Nancy was abducted by the Lord's Resistance Army (LRA) when she was nine years old. After being taken to the bush, she was forced into being a "babysitter" of one of the head commanders. If she did not do things correctly, according to his rules, she was beaten terribly.

After six years, Nancy was trained as a soldier and taught to fight. She attempted to escape but got caught in crossfire between the LRA and the Ugandan Police Defense Force (UPDF). She found herself in a pool of blood after being shot in the jaw and face. Nancy was ultimately found and taken by the UPDF soldiers to Gulu Support the Children Organization (GUSCO), where she was sent to a hospital and fed through a tube for six months. After her recovery she went to St. Monica's Tailoring School for Girls in Gulu. During a trip to visit her mother, whom she hadn't seen for years due to the war, a Ugandan soldier took advantage of her and she ended up pregnant. The man never claimed the baby and as result of her pregnancy and deformity, her family ostracized her, including her own mother. Nancy and her 10-month-old daughter, Peace, remain at St. Monica's. The school provides her with day care, housing, meals, and an education, with the intention of helping her gain the independence to one day support herself.

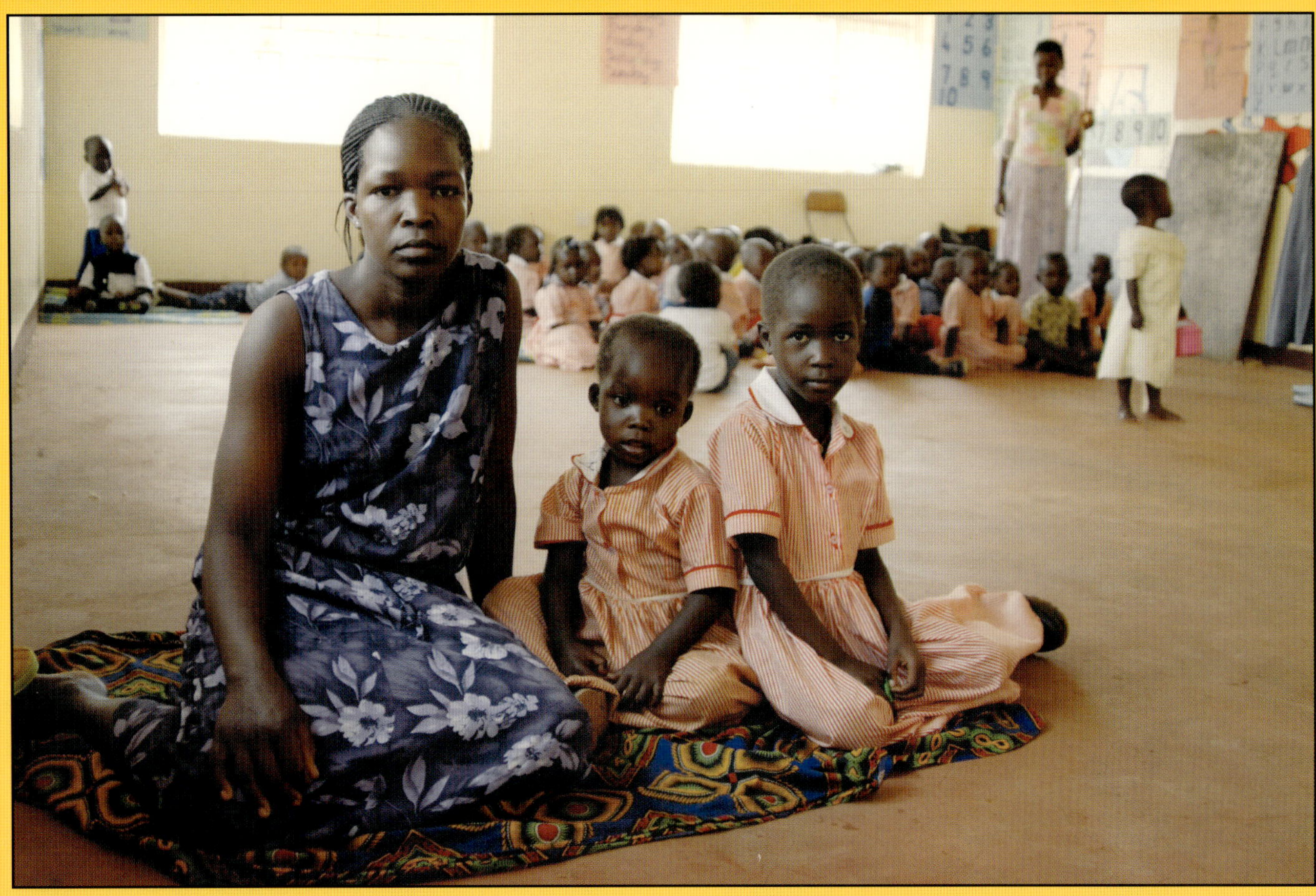

Photograph by Riccardo Gangale

Rose was 10 years old when she was abducted by the LRA on her way to visit her grandmother. She was raped, beaten, and passed from one soldier to another. She gave birth to her first child at the age of 15. After the baby was born, she felt there was no way to escape. Rose continued fighting as a child soldier, all the while enduring severe trauma. She gave birth to two more children.

After the third child, Rose decided to try and escape. Two of the children were walking by then, and the third one was tied to her back. Her escape was successful and she was taken in by GUSCO. She remained there for one year. Eventually, a missionary worker took her out and brought her to Lacor hospital for rehabilitation. During that time, no relatives came to claim her. She was given a small hut in an IDP camp with her three children and then brought to St. Monica's. Her trauma had been so severe that she even attempted to kill her children several times—her eldest daughter reported "Many times my mother tries to burn us with fire." After four years at St. Monica's, Rose has learned to sew very well and gets paid for what she produces. Her children are in the day care nursery, and through the constant care and support she has received from St Monica's she has been able to love her children in a healthy way. Through love, work, and education, Rose has begun to heal from the extreme trauma she endured during the war.

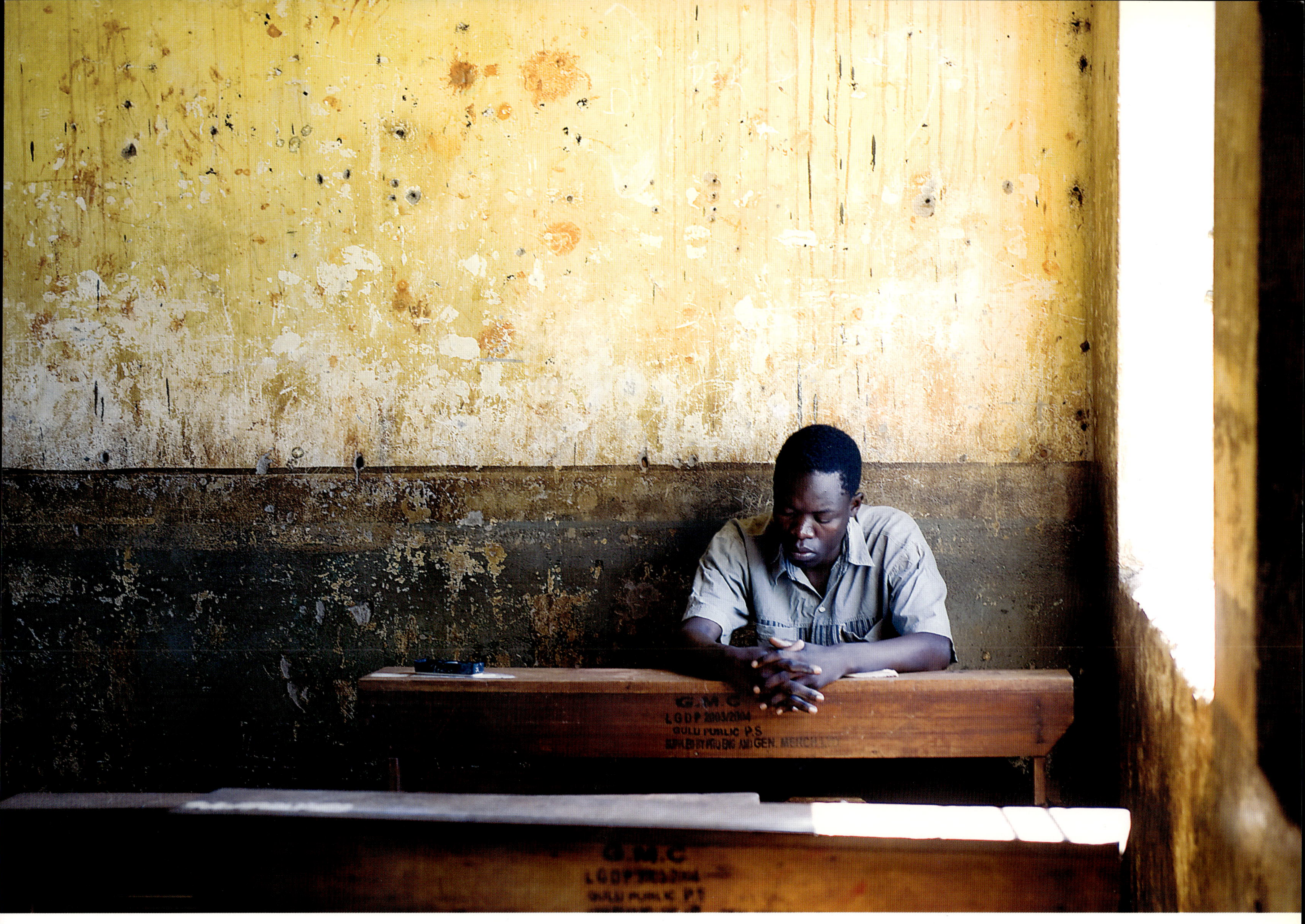

This rehabilitation center sponsors the education of former child soldiers who bore the brunt of atrocities committed by the LRA.
Photograph by Heather McClintock

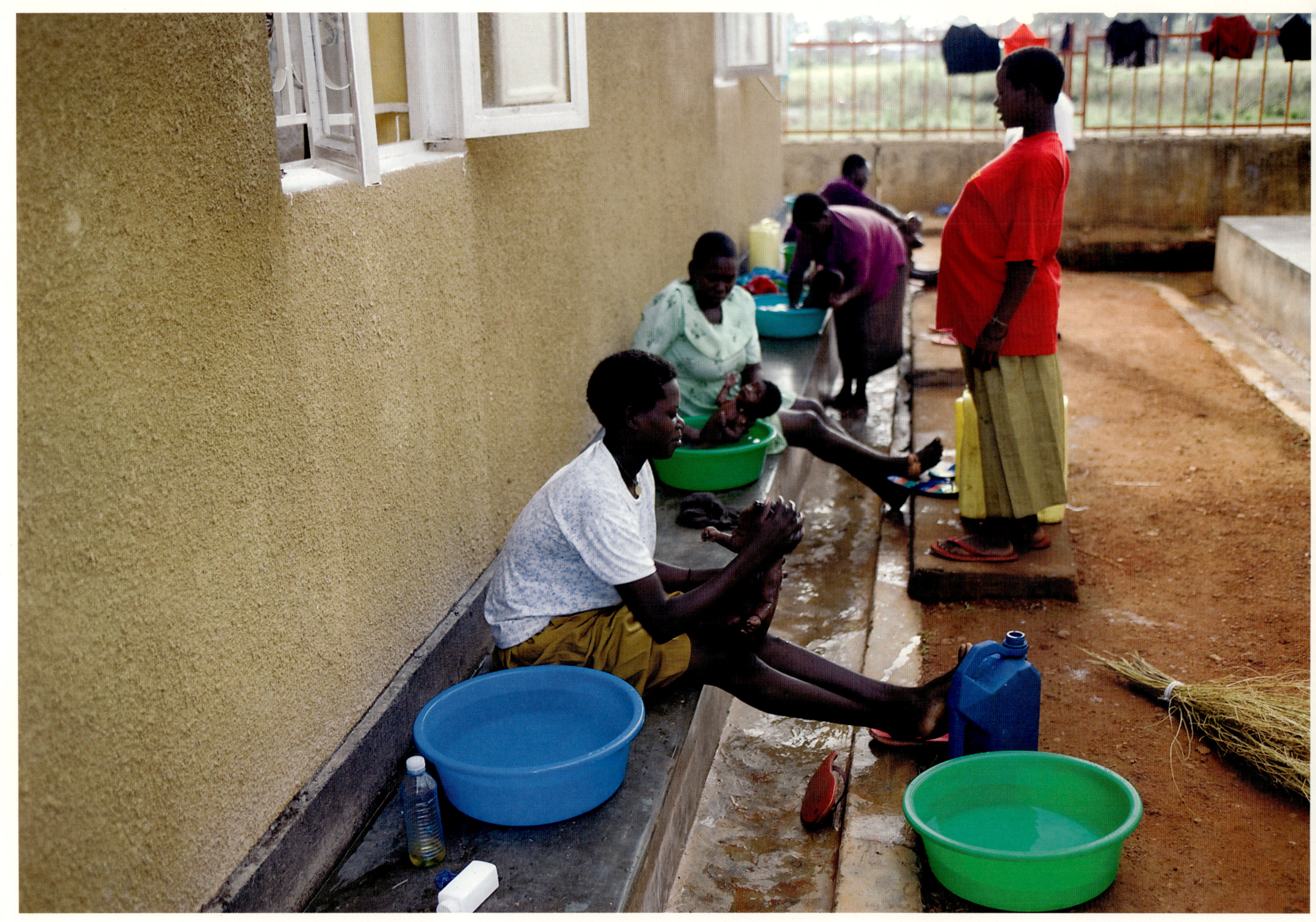

Former child "wives" at a rehabilitation center bathe their babies. Every pregnancy and baby at the Rachel Rehabilitation Center (RRC) was the product of an LRA rape. Photograph by Heather McClintock

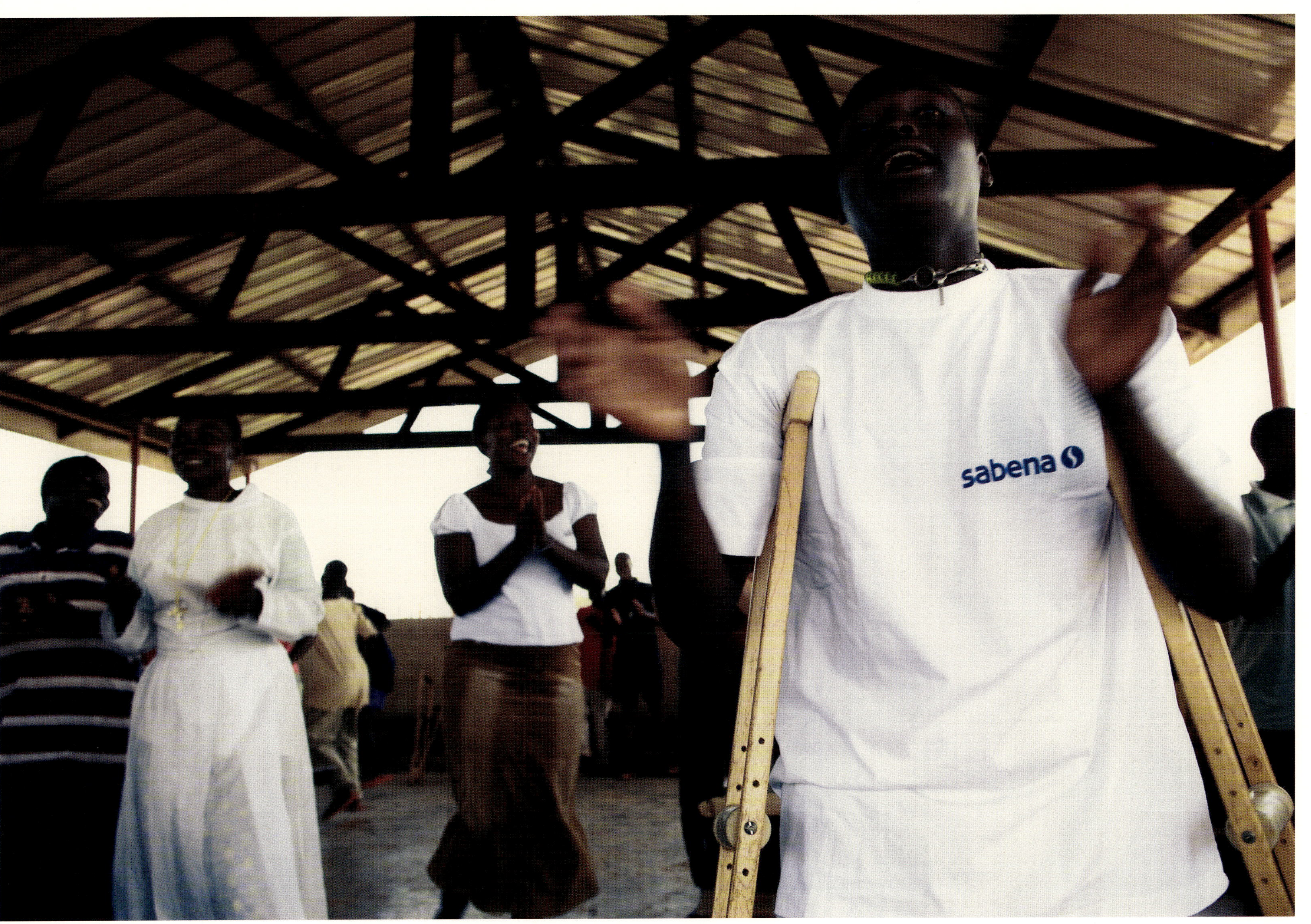

At a rehabilitation center, to encourage recovery, children talk about their experiences in captivity and express their feelings through church services, music, drama, and drawings. Photograph by Heather McClintock

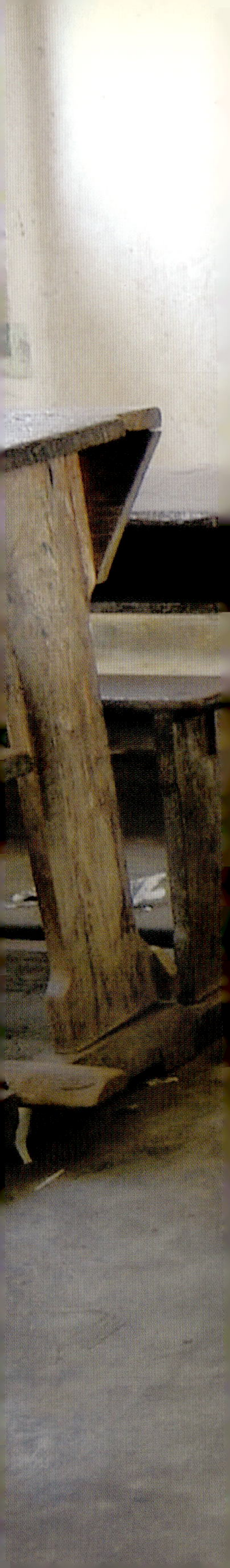

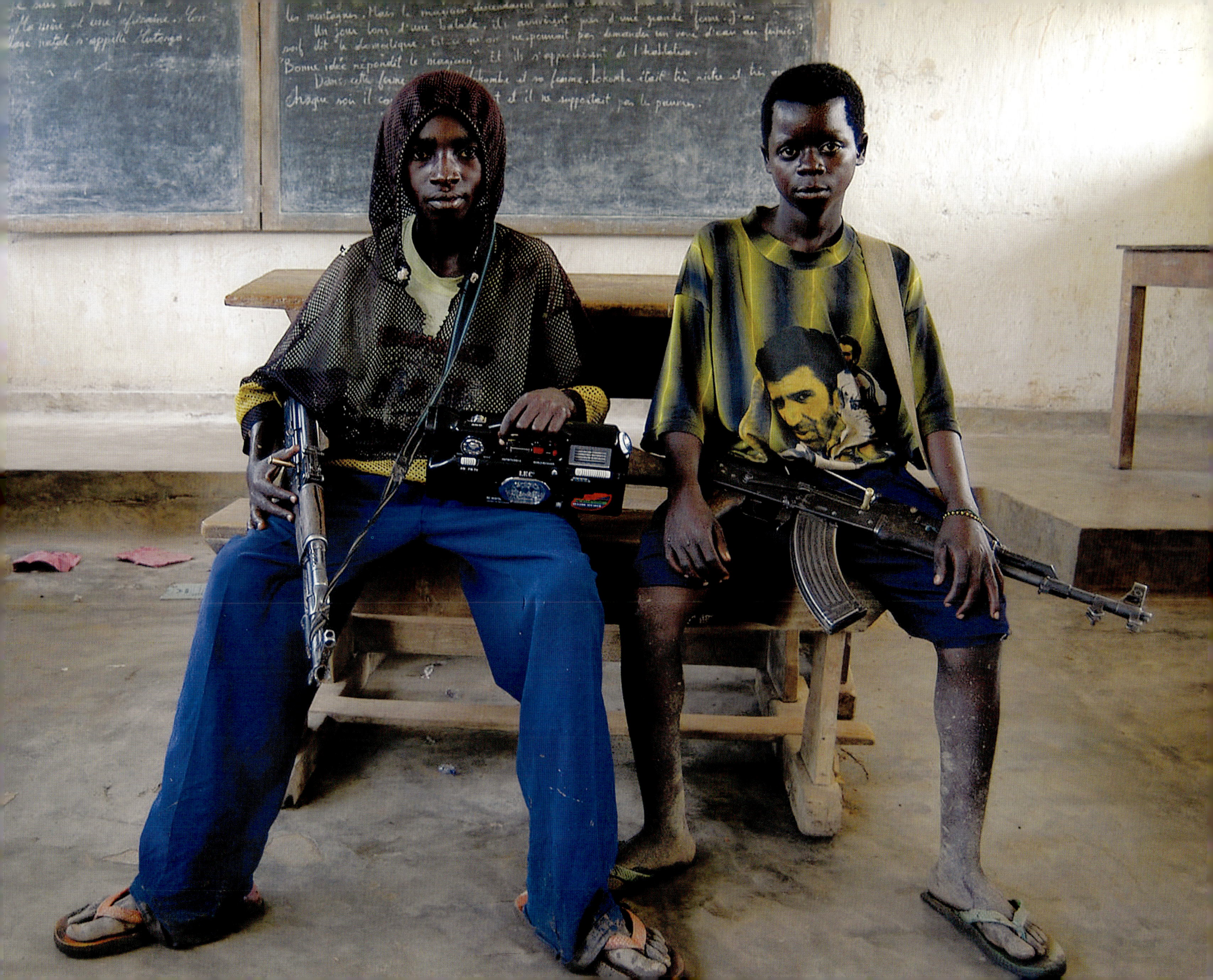

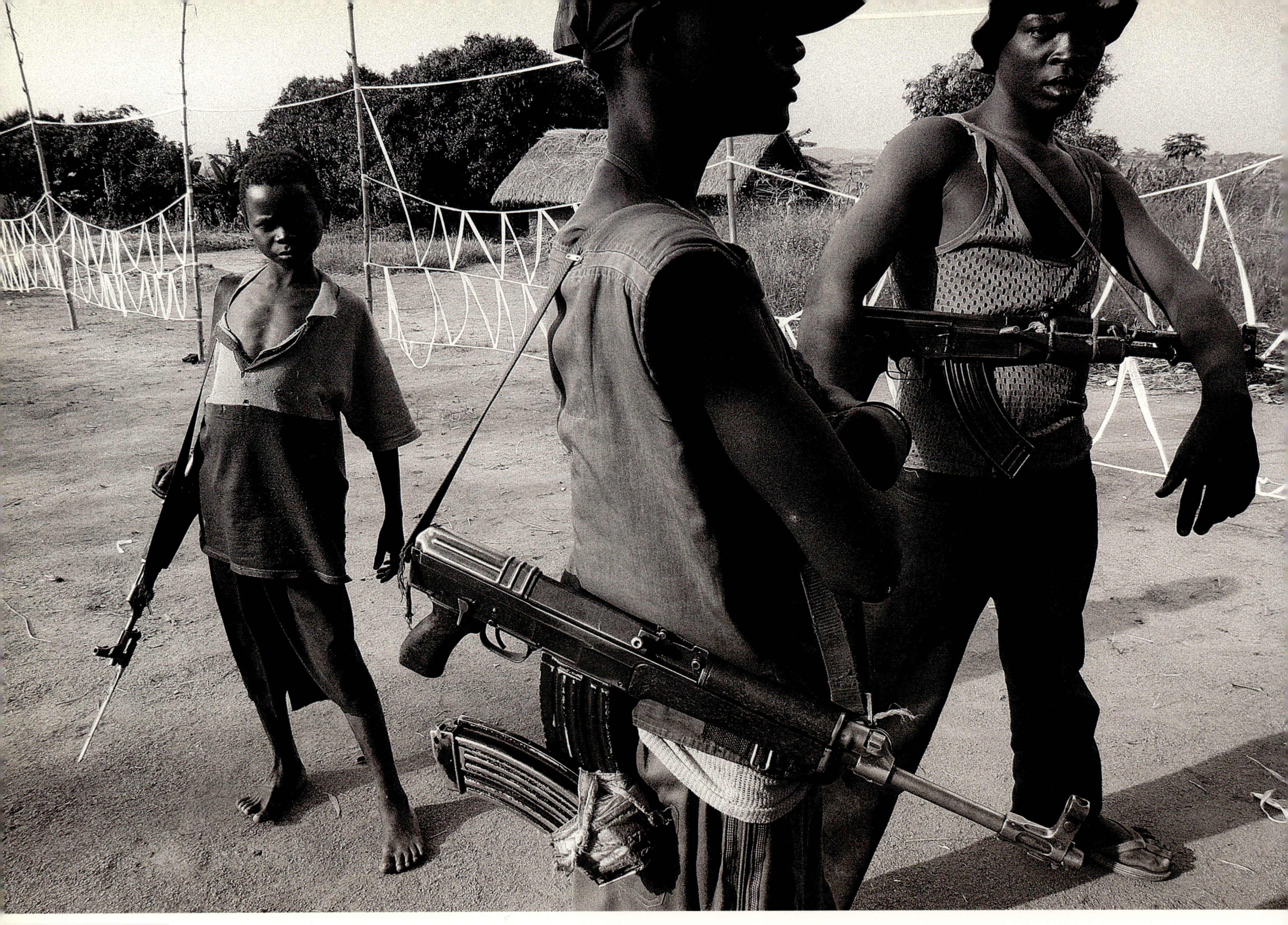

A small boy, an adolescent, and a young man bear arms in the same Lendu militia unit. They stand on the road between Bunia and Marabou, where killings occur regularly. Photograph by Roger Lemoyne

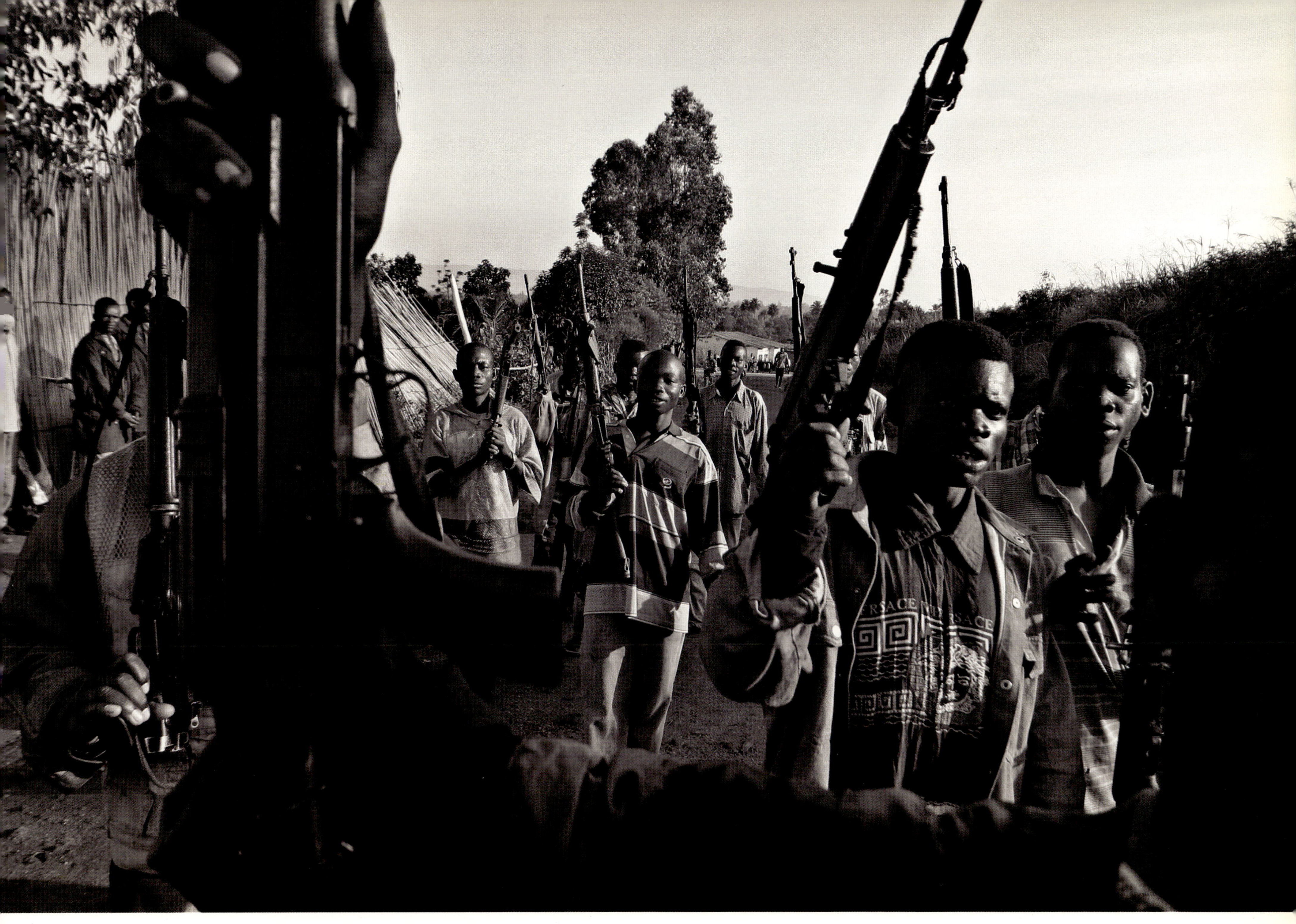

Child militias turn in their weapons to the United Nations Peace Keeping Mission to the Congo before joining.
Photograph by Roger Lemoyne

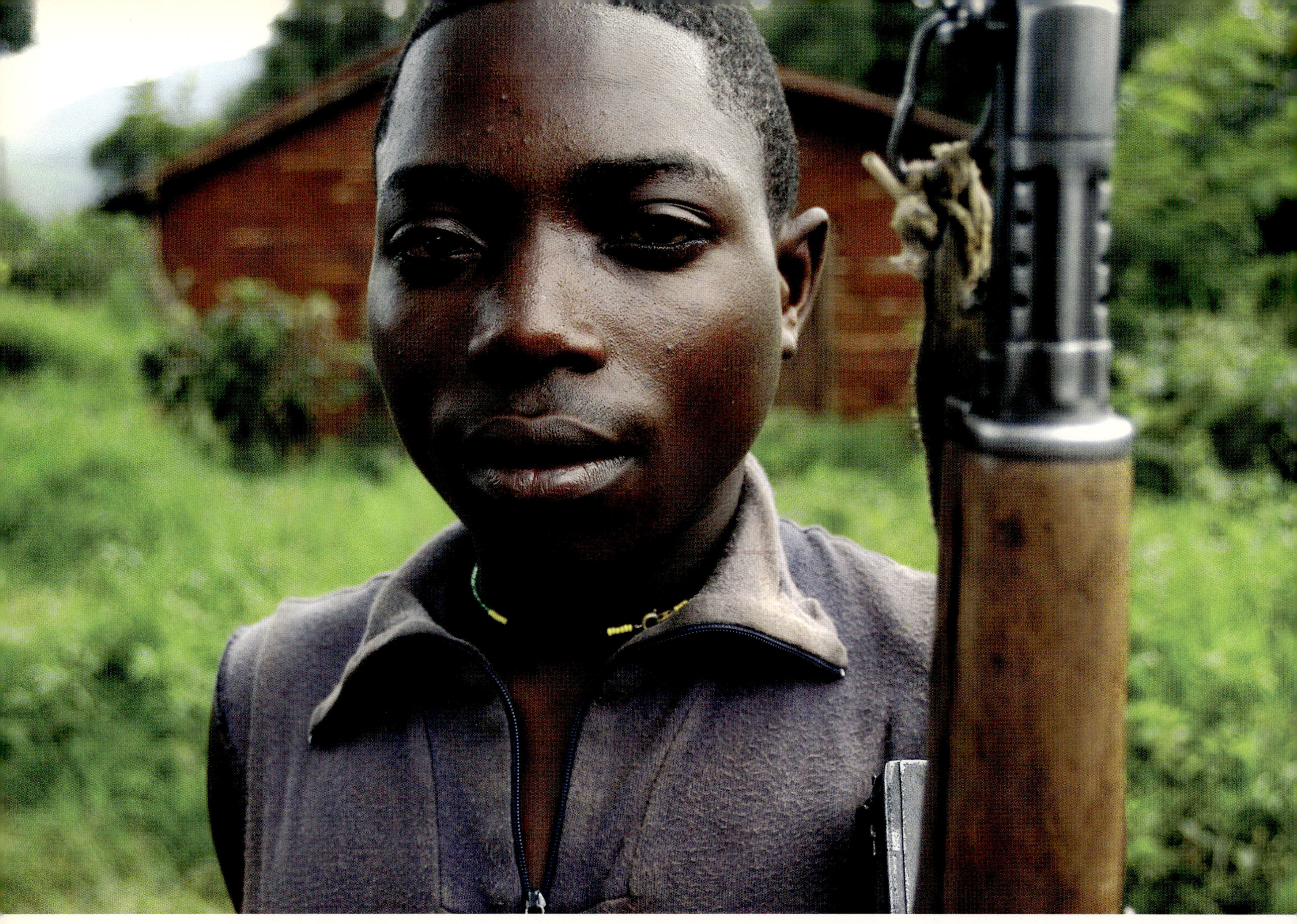

A boy fighter from a former militia stands outside a military post while waiting to be integrated into the new Congolese army.
Photograph by Riccardo Gangale

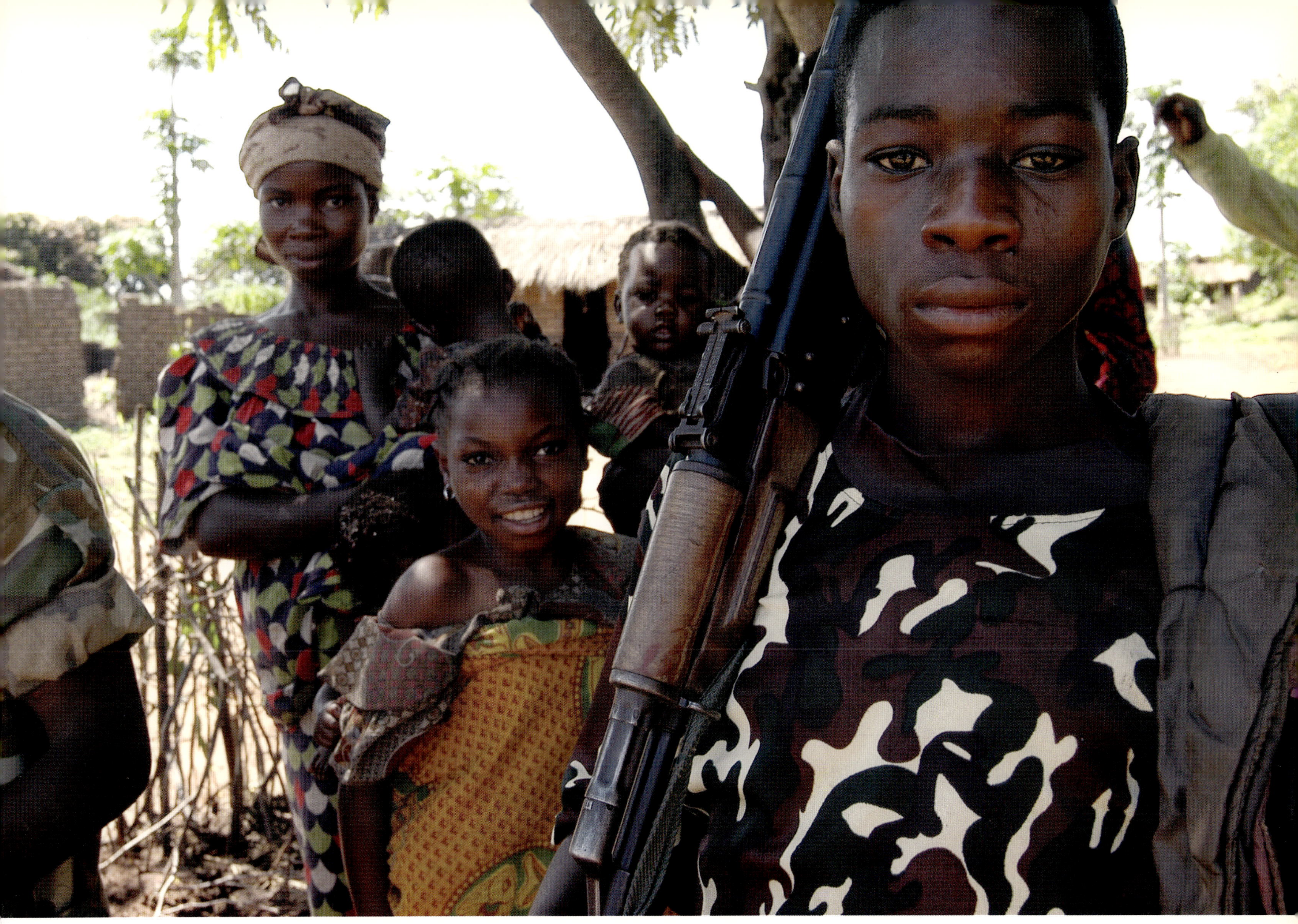

A child Mai Mai soldier waits for training in South Kivu Province. Photograph by Riccardo Gangale

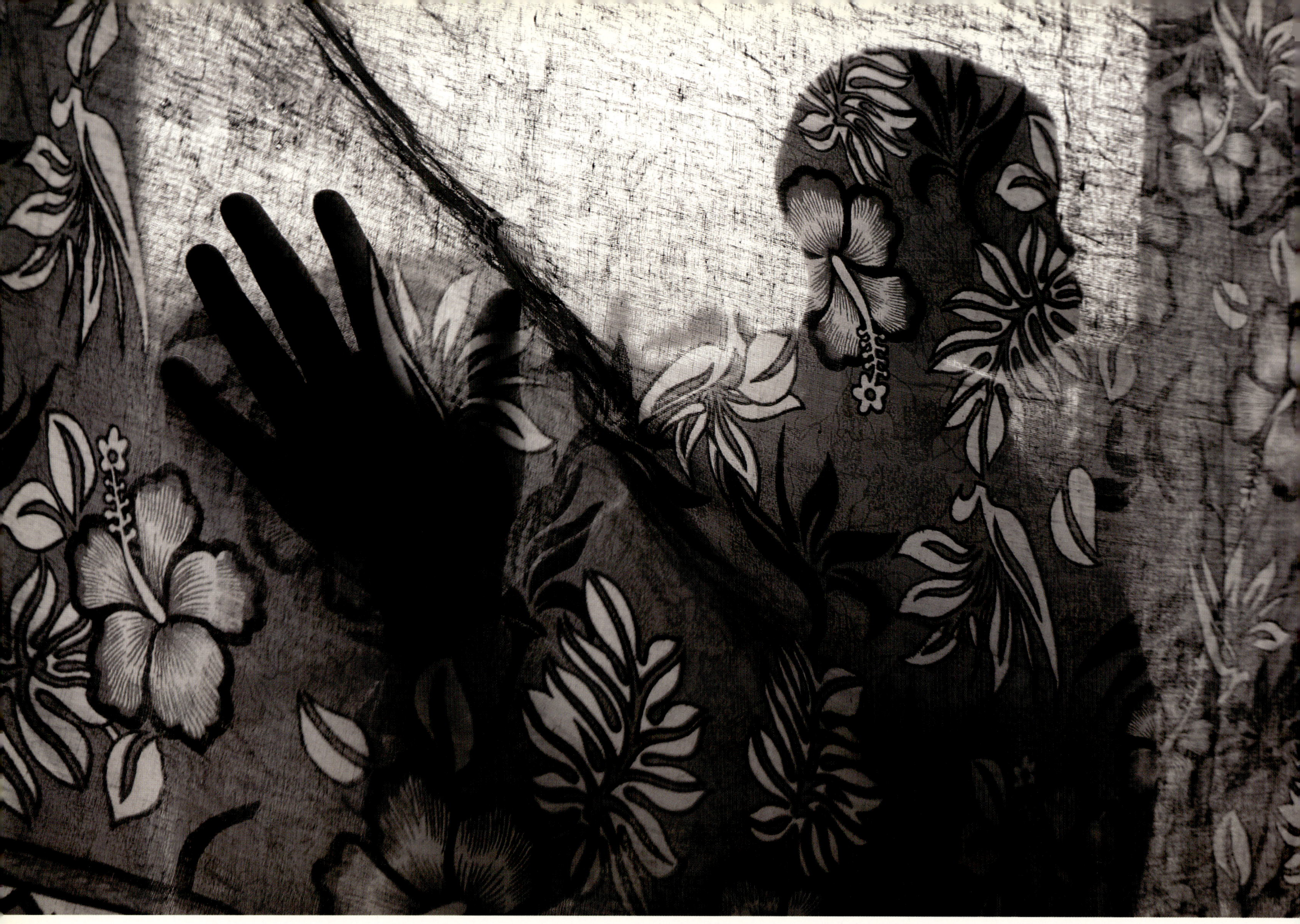

Above: A girl, taken as a commander's "wife," stands behind a curtain in a local hospital, waiting to be examined for sexually transmitted diseases. Right: An 11-year-old boy, recently demobilized, sits in a dormitory run by UNICEF in the DRC. Photographs by Roger Lemoyne

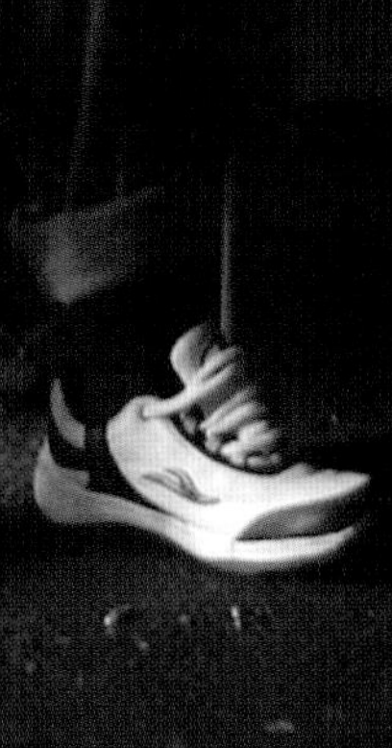
unicef
unicef
unicef

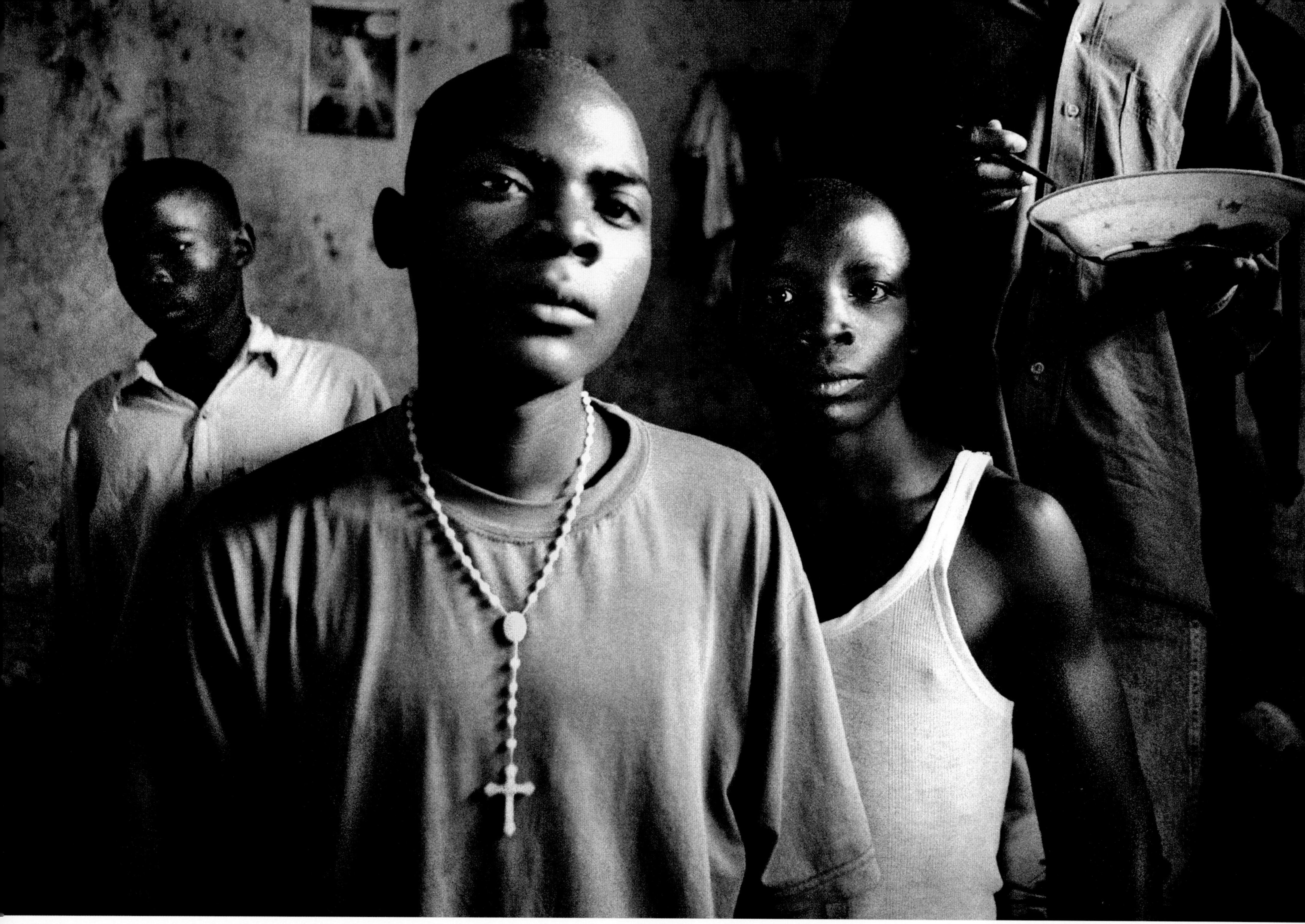

This prison houses many former child soldiers. Photograph by Cedric Gerbehaye

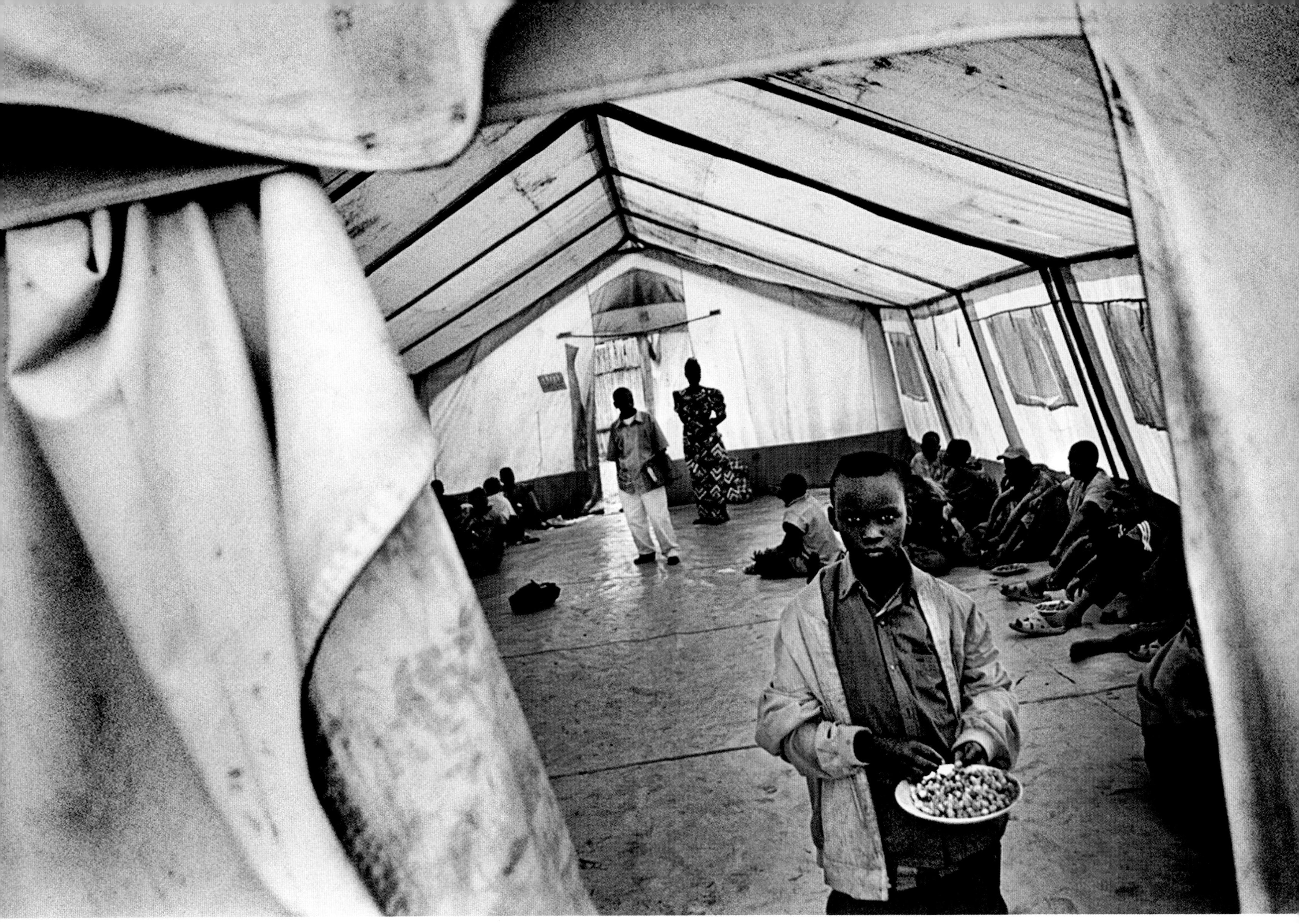

A former child fighter at a transit camp in the DRC. Photograph by Cedric Gerbehaye

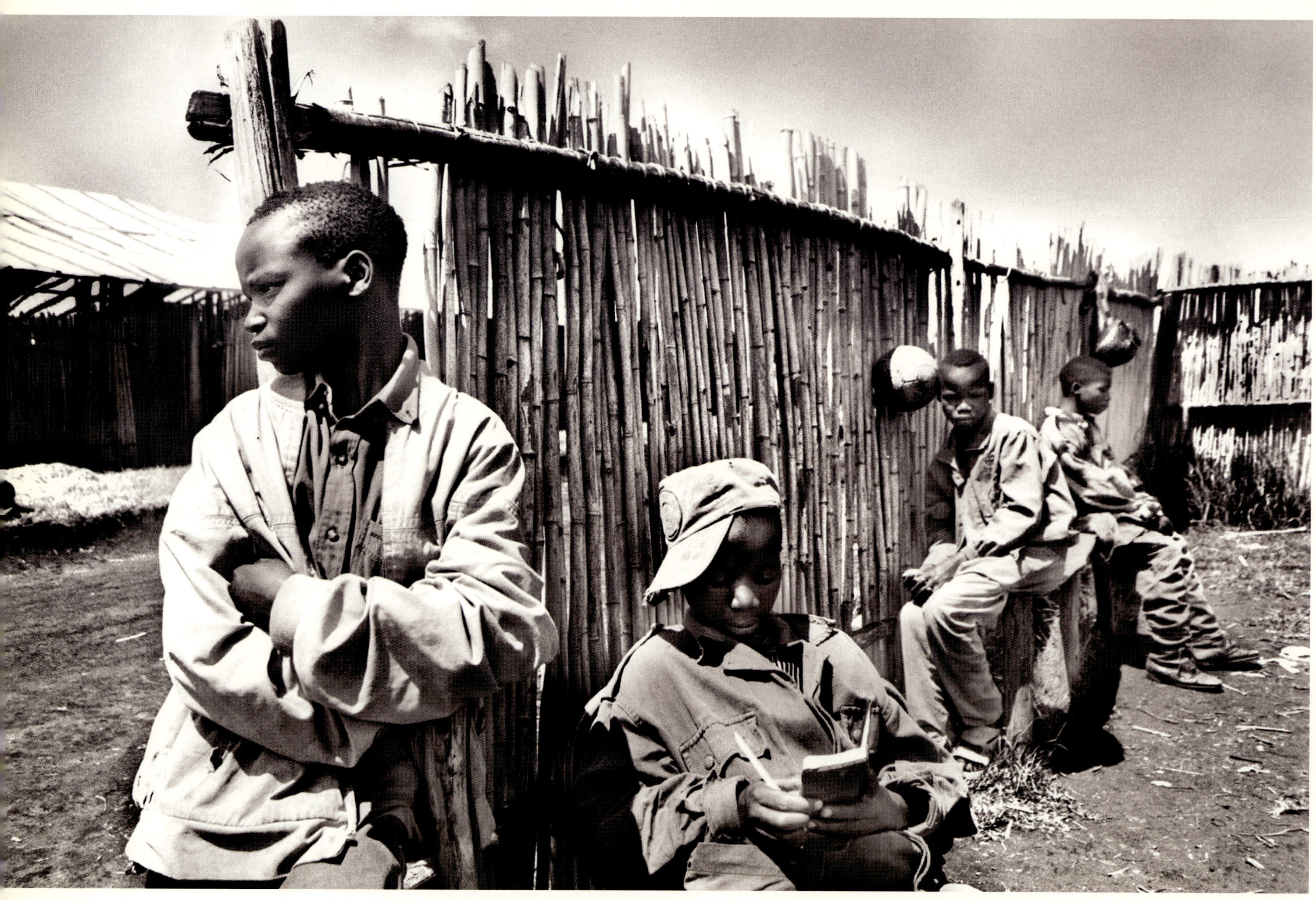

Above: Child soldiers from the Nationalist and Integrationist Front (FNI) wait at a transit camp the day after their demobilization.
Right: A recently demobilized former child fighter stands outside a transit camp in the DRC. Photographs by Cedric Gerbehaye

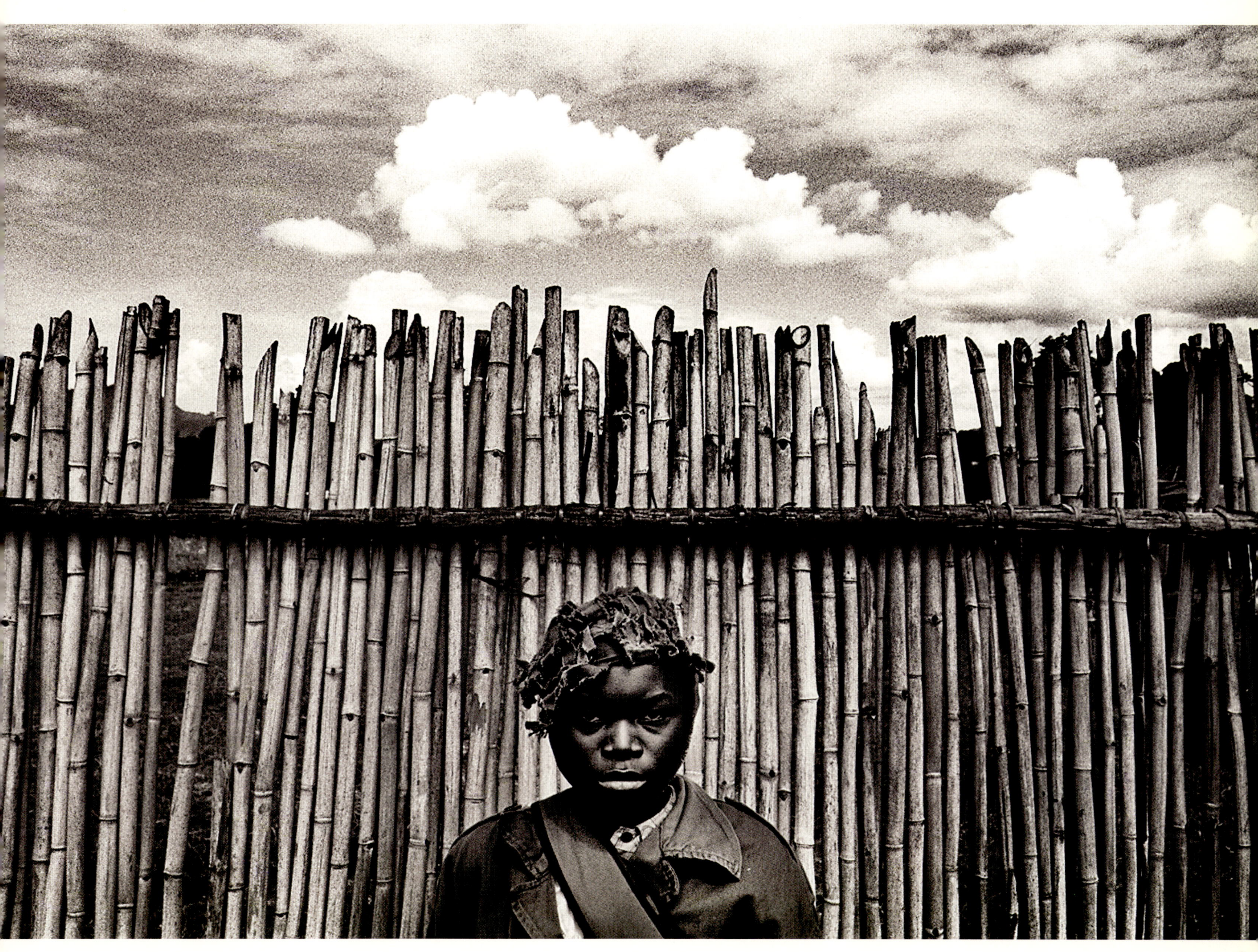

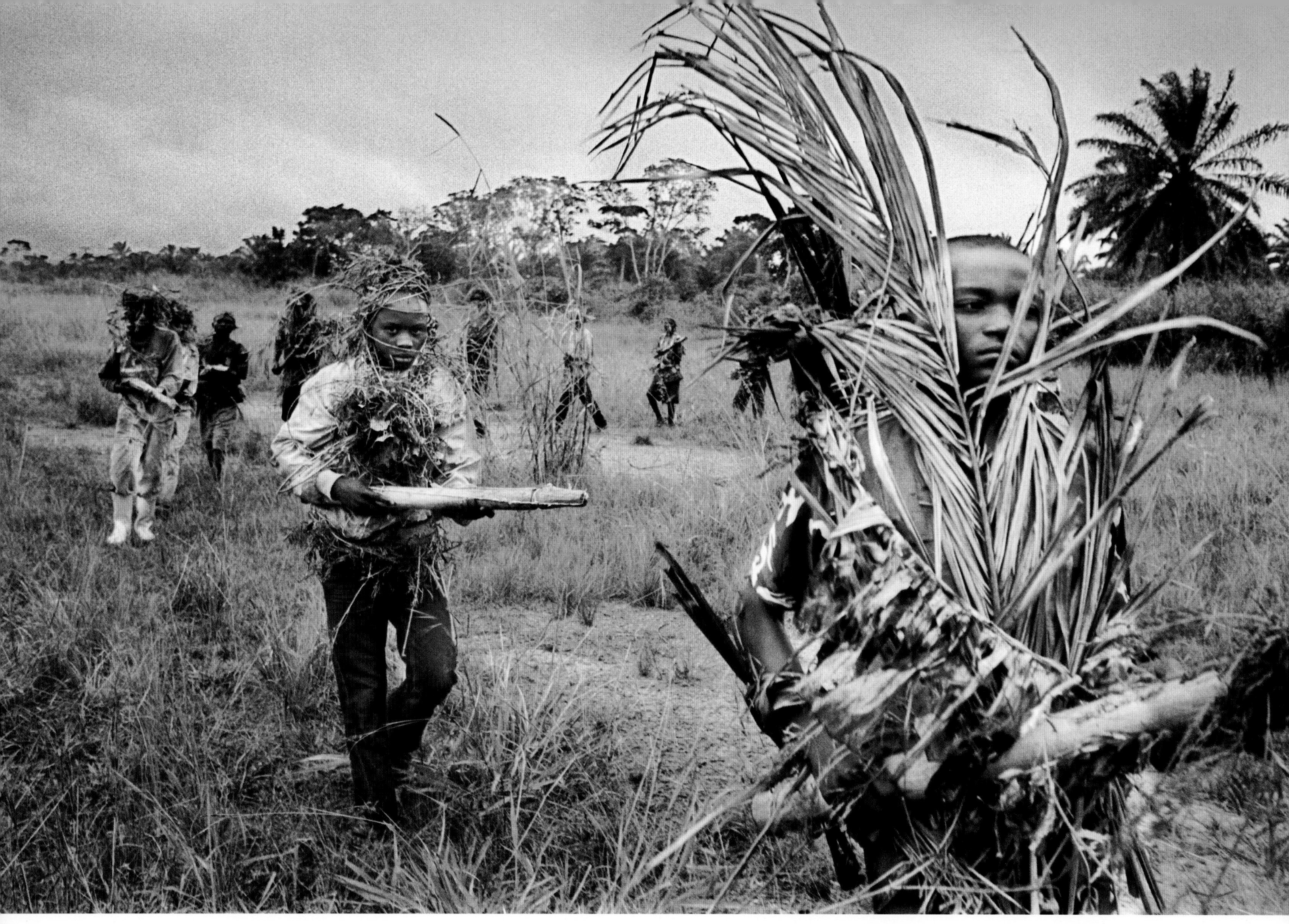

Training camp for Mai-Mai soldiers in Beni, an eastern province in the Congo. Photograph by Guy Tillim/Agence VU

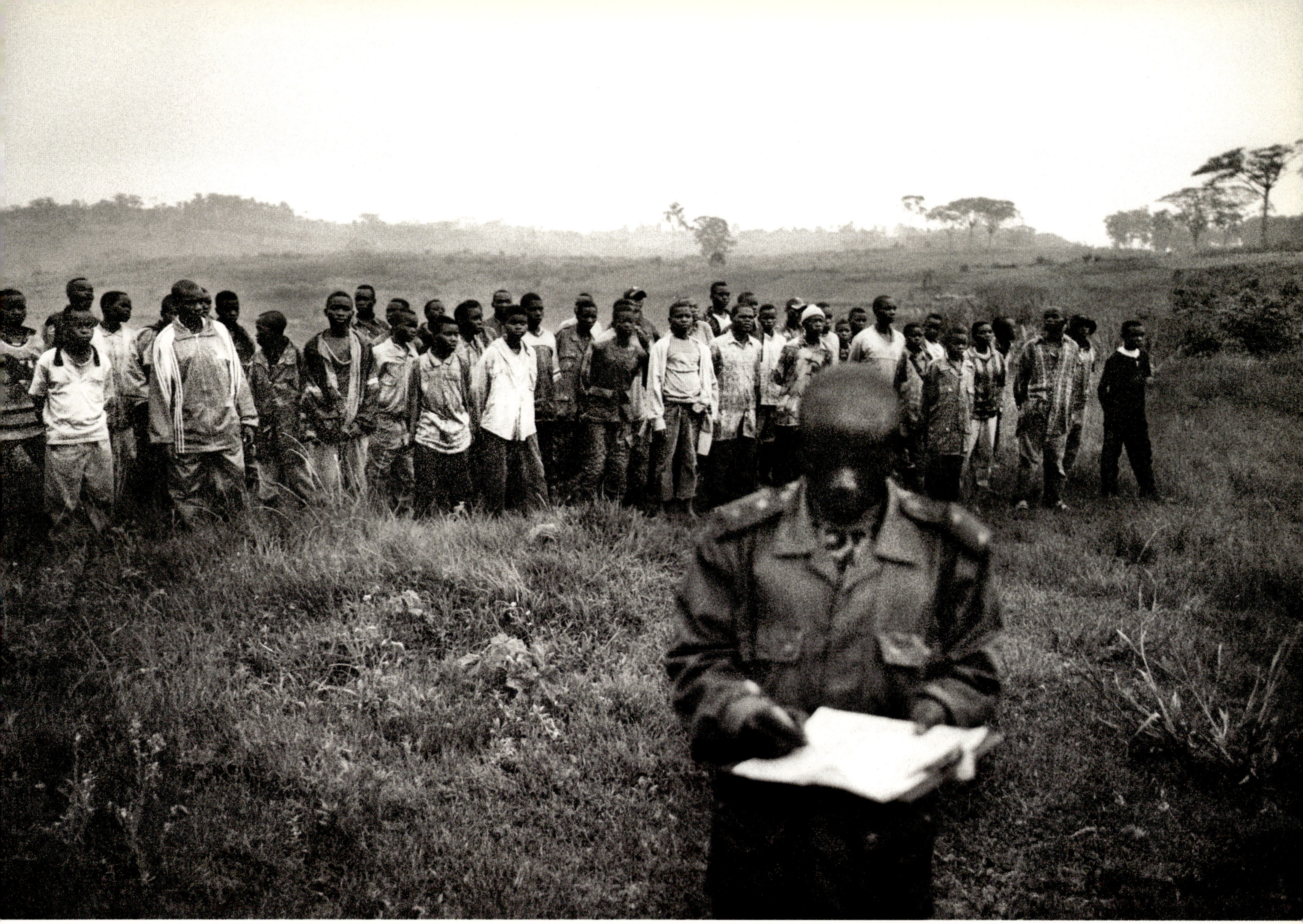

A demobilization transit camp for FNI rebels at Kpandroma, in the Ituri district. The demobilized rebels must choose between rehabilitation and joining the FARDC, the government forces they had been fighting until demobilization. Photograph by Cedric Gerbehaye

africa: liberia

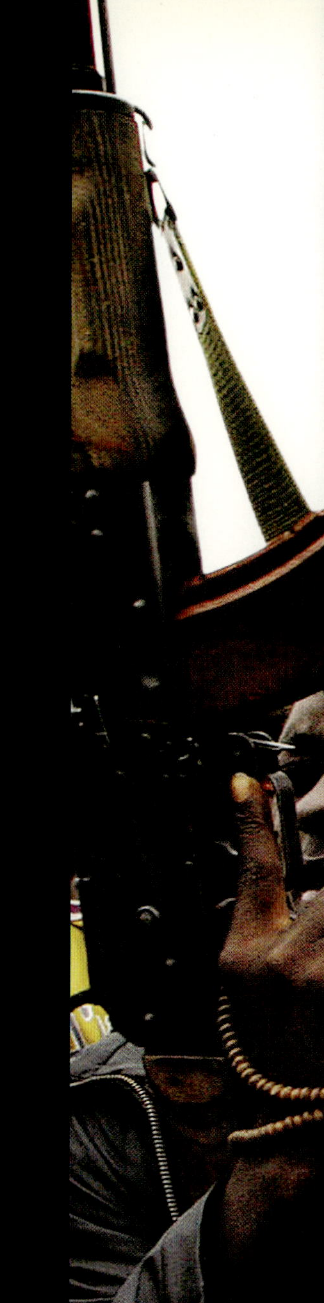

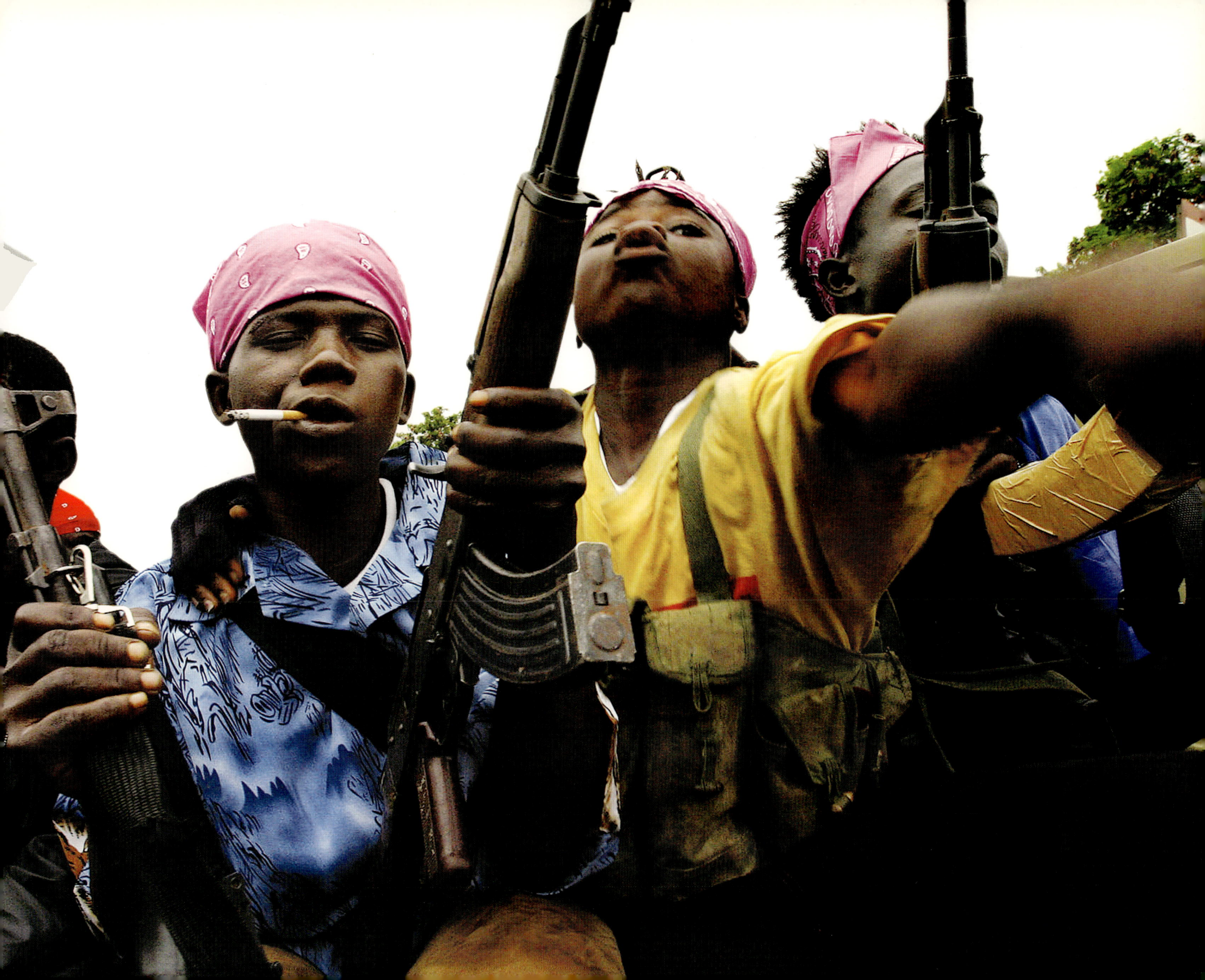

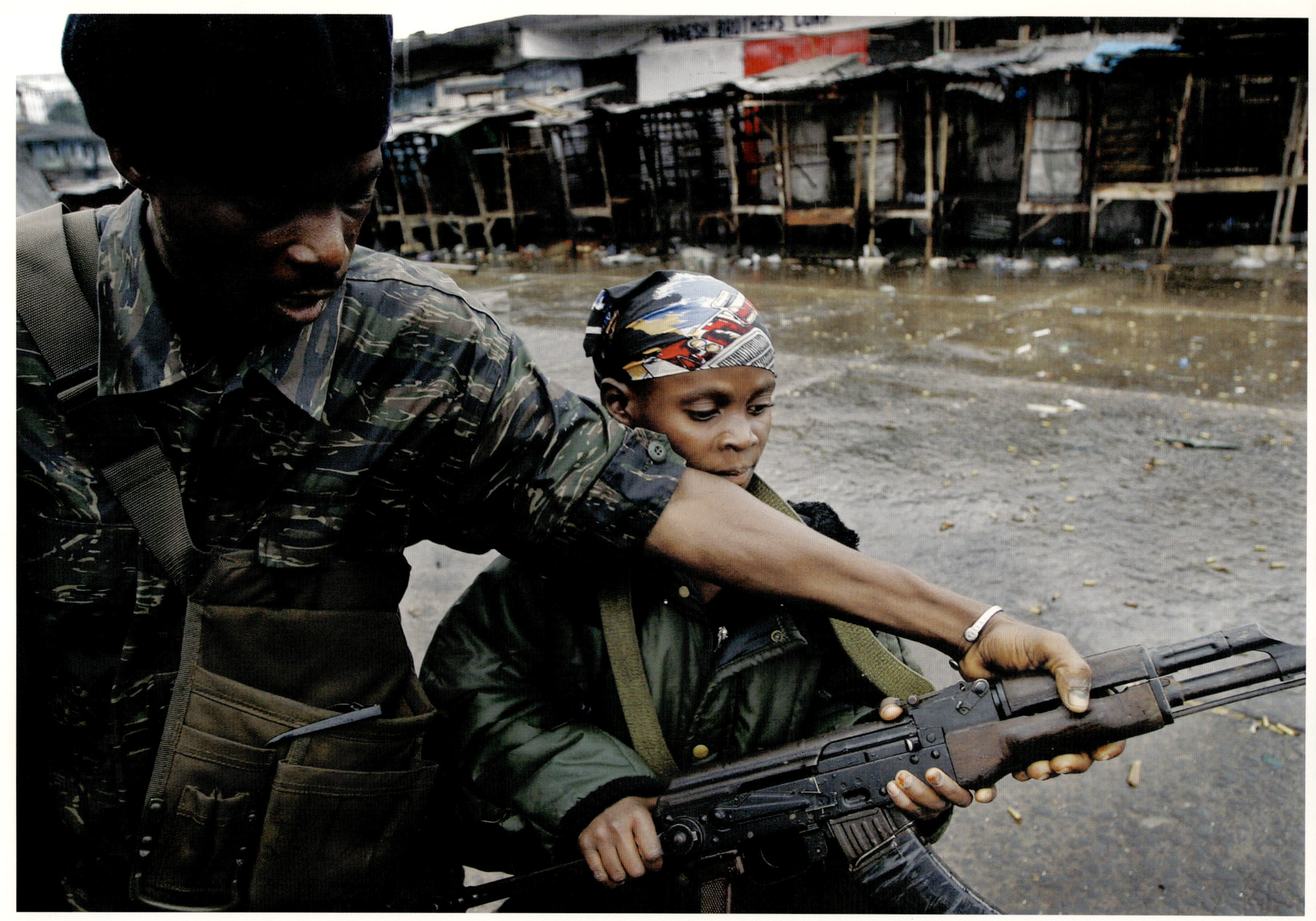

A government soldier shows an 11-year-old how to handle an AK-47. Photograph by Q. Sakamaki

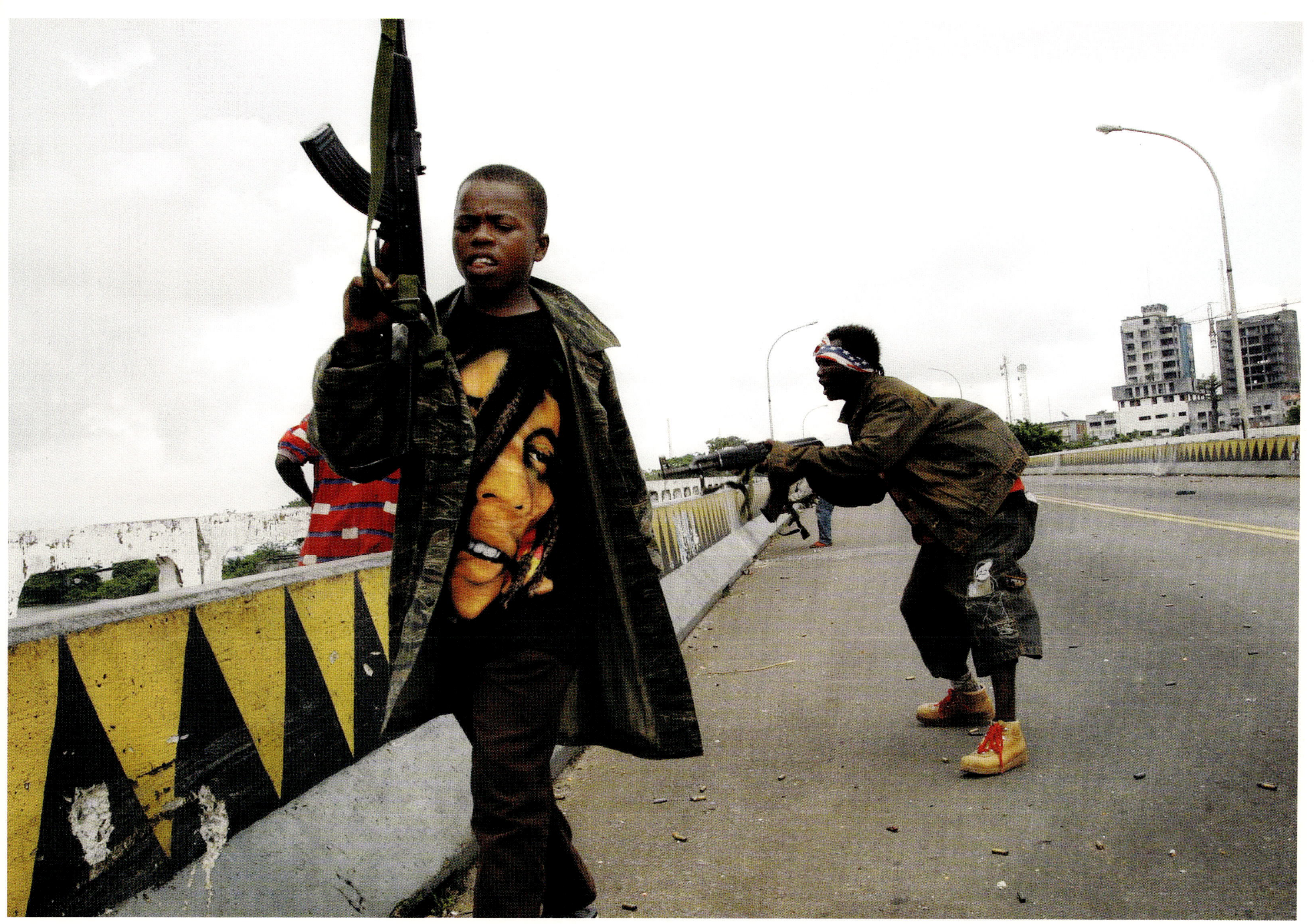

While under fire from the Liberians United for Reconciliation and Democracy (LURD), a young boy fighting for the Liberian government defiantly walks toward the incoming bullets. He and his friend fire AK-47s to push back the rebel group's advances. Photograph by Q. Sakamaki

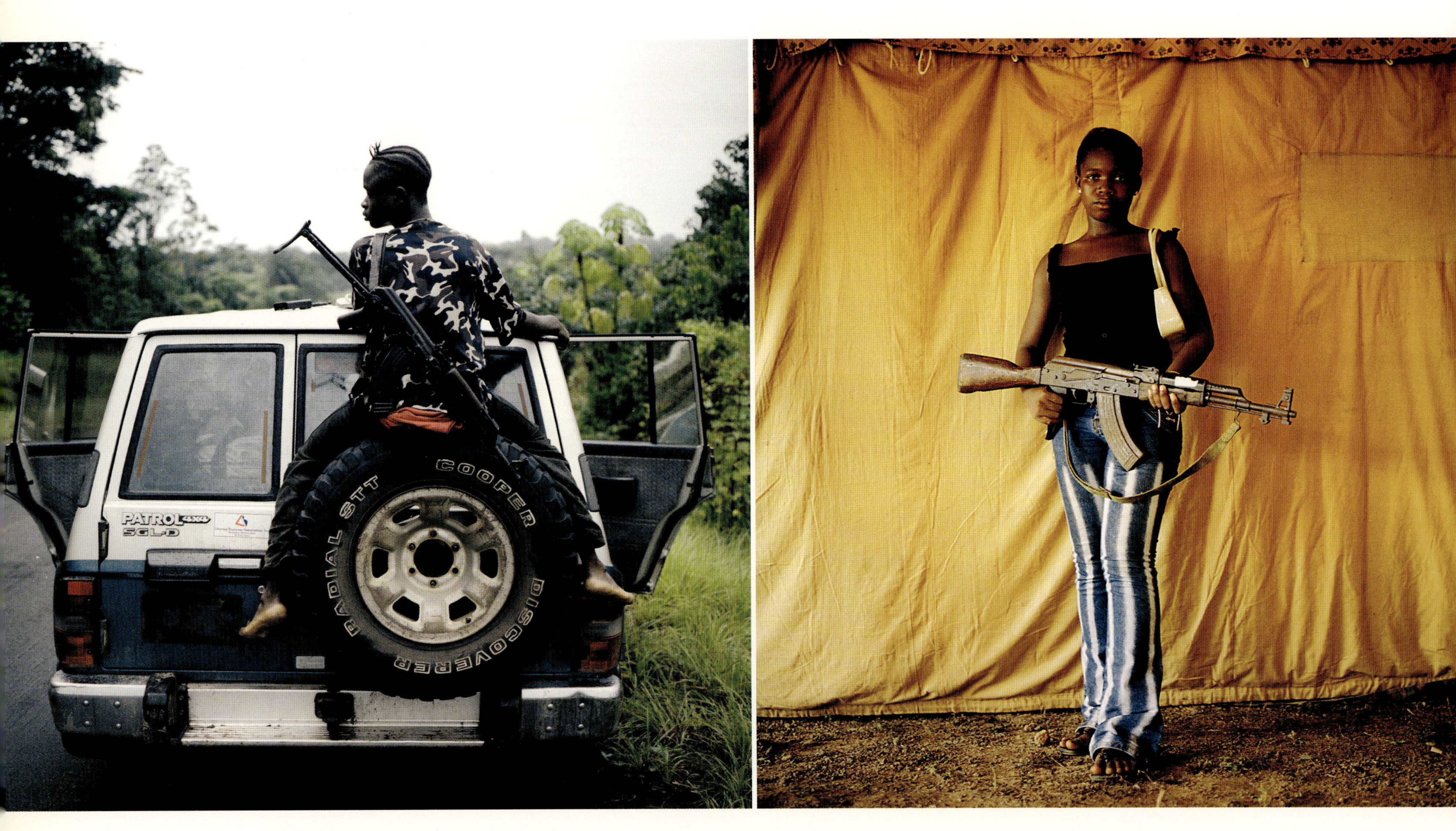

Above left: Photograph by Tim A. Hetherington. Above right: Sierra Leonian girl fighter with the LURD poses with her weapon at a UN disarmament point. Photograph by Tim A. Hetherington. Right: Former soldiers, militia members, and child soldiers hand over their weapons and ammunition to the UN. Photograph by Sven Torfinn

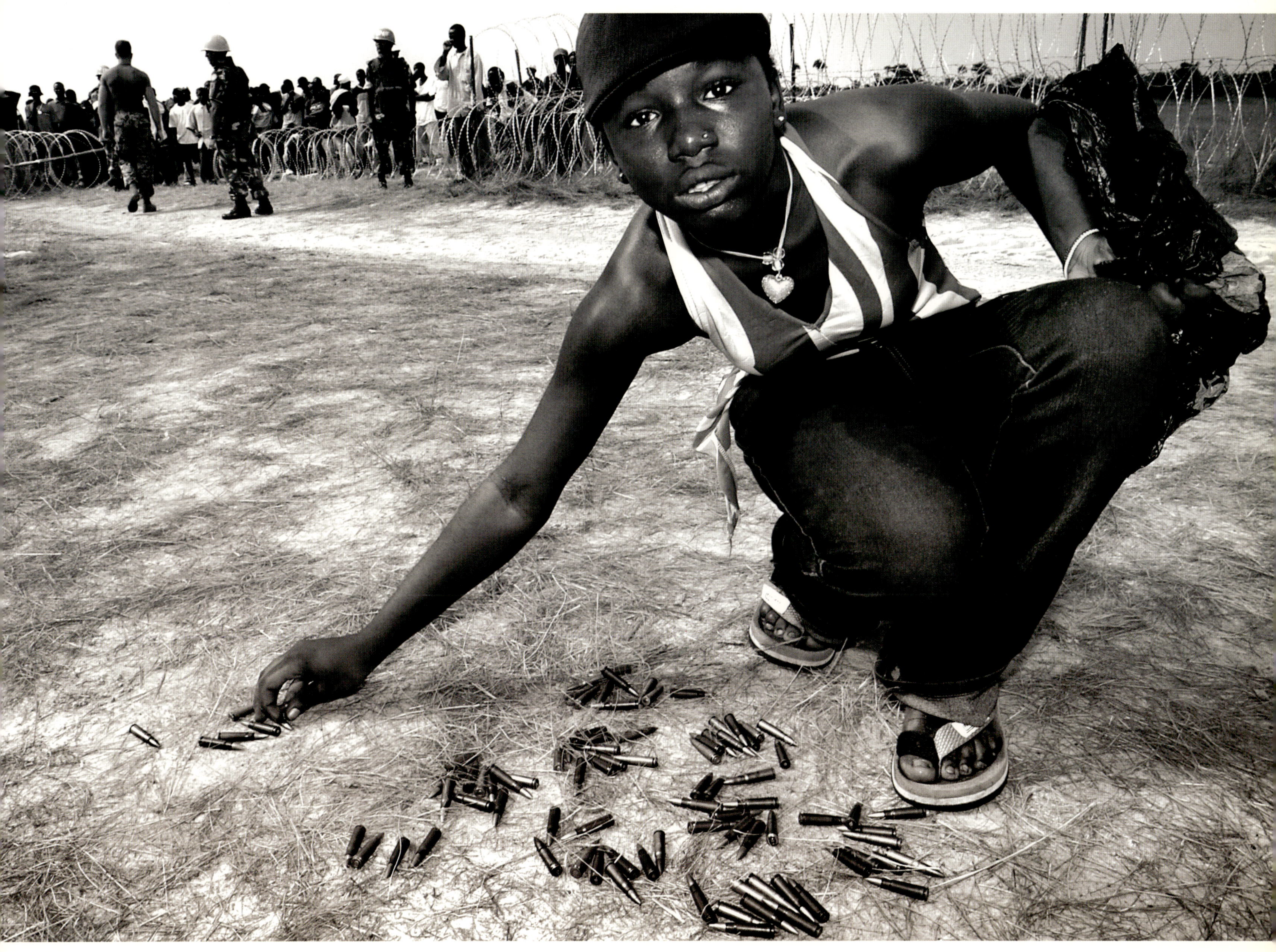

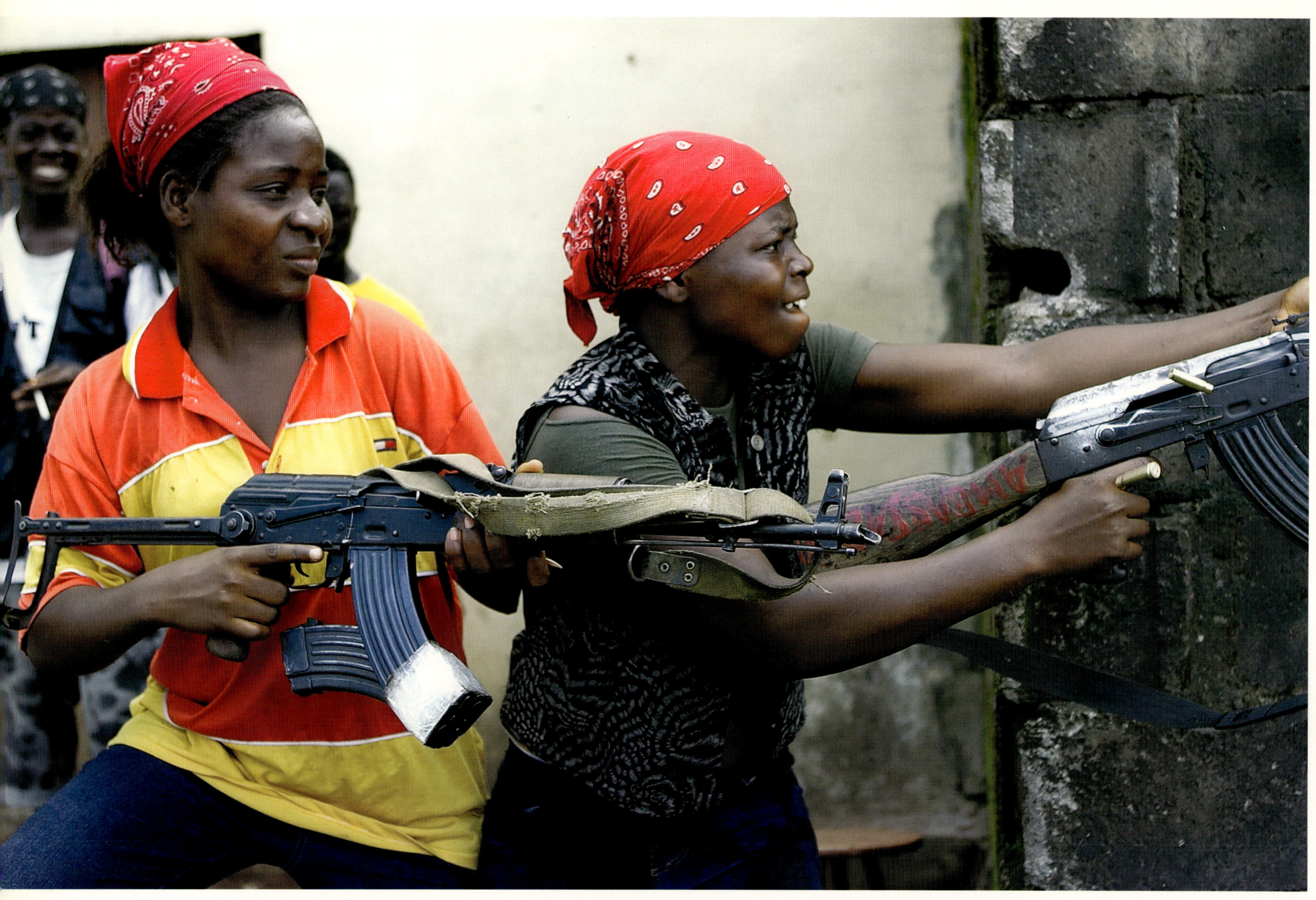

Above: Two young girls fight in the streets of Monrovia for the government militia. Photograph by Richard Butler. Right: A young LURD fighter smokes a cigarette near the hilltop compound of the LURD chairman, Sekou Conneh. The chairman's image appears on the boy's t-shirt. Photograph by Tim A. Hetherington

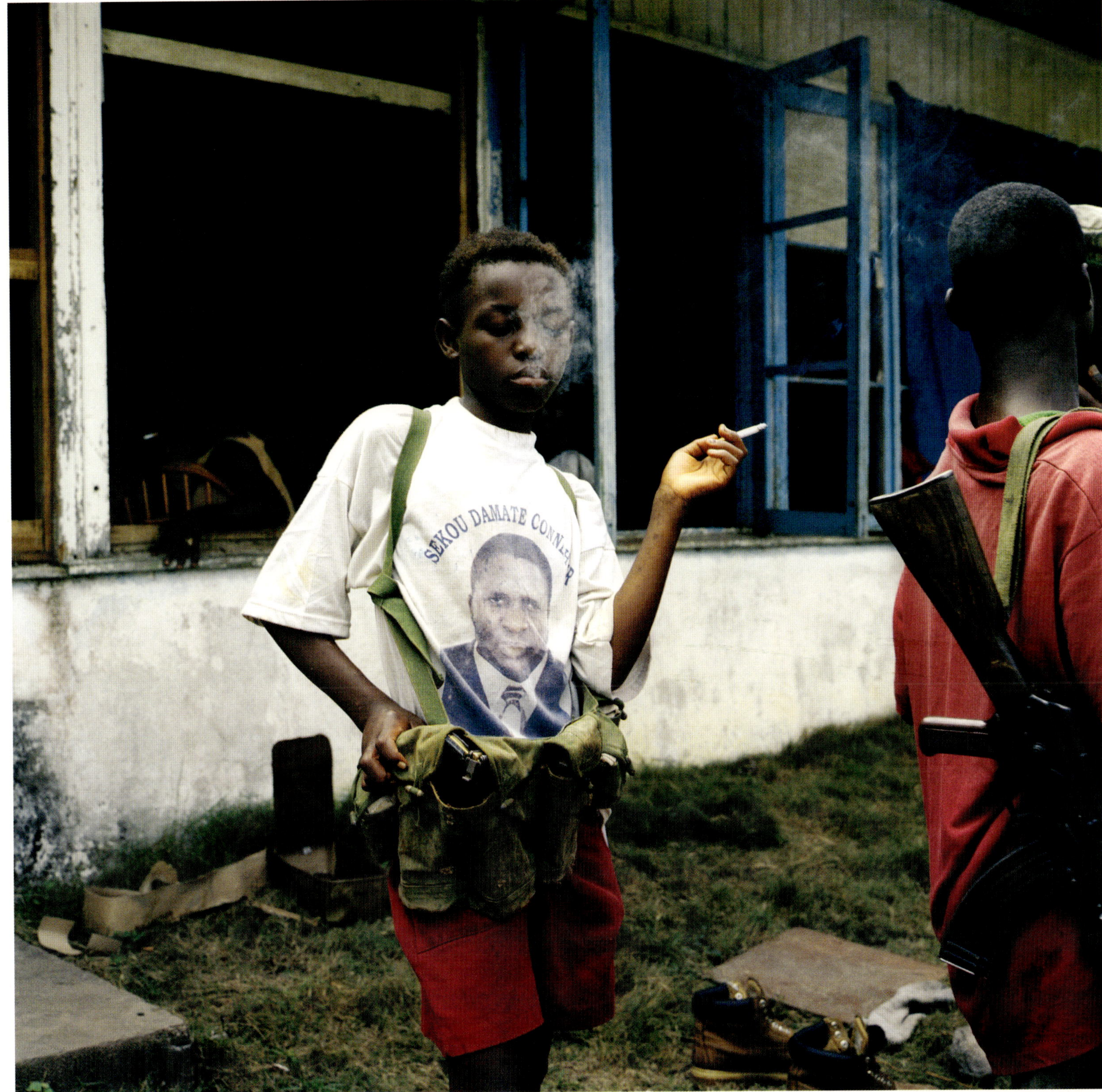
SEKOU DAMATE

africa: sierra leone

An 11-year-old Civil Defense Forces (CDF) soldier, Kono State, Sierra Leone.
Photograph by Guy Tillim

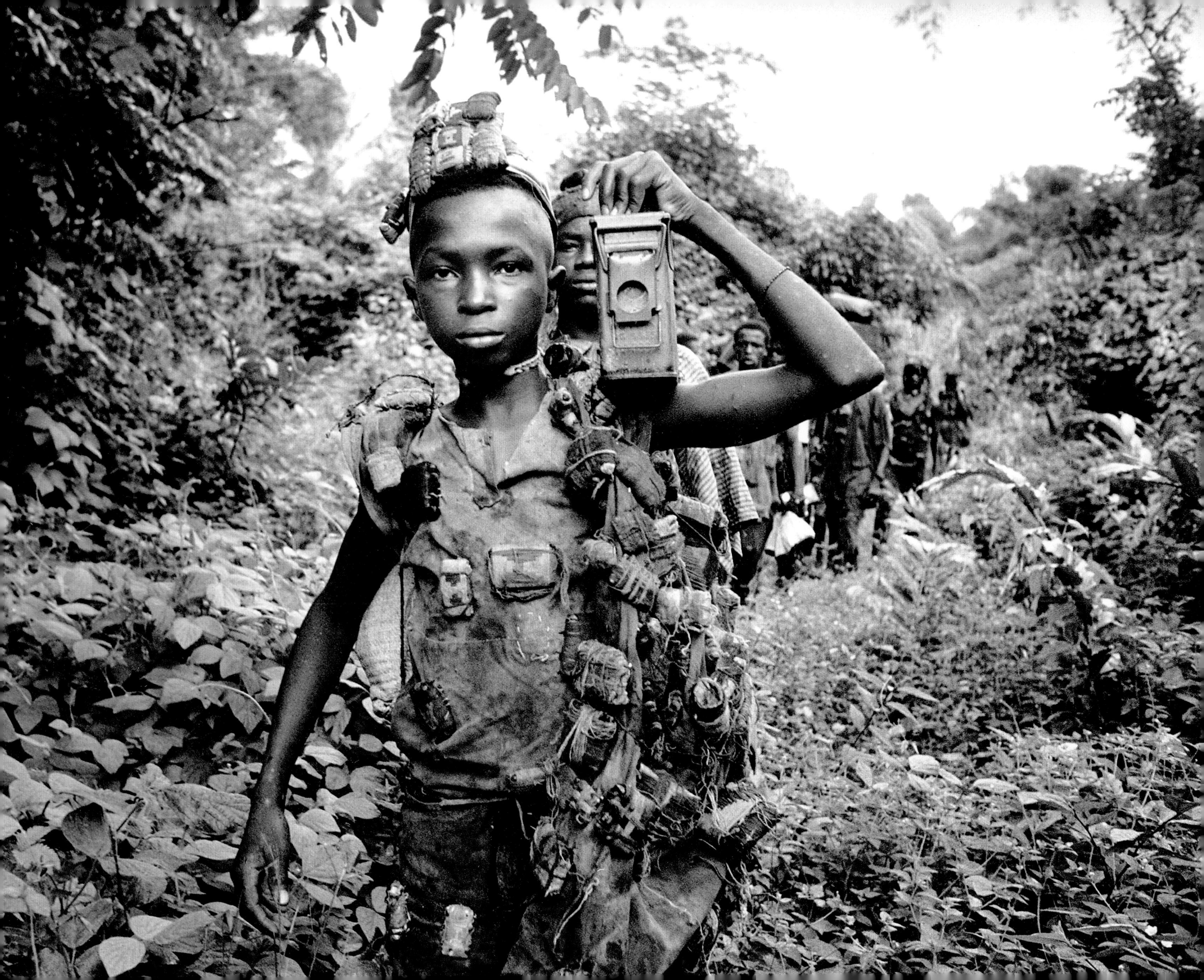

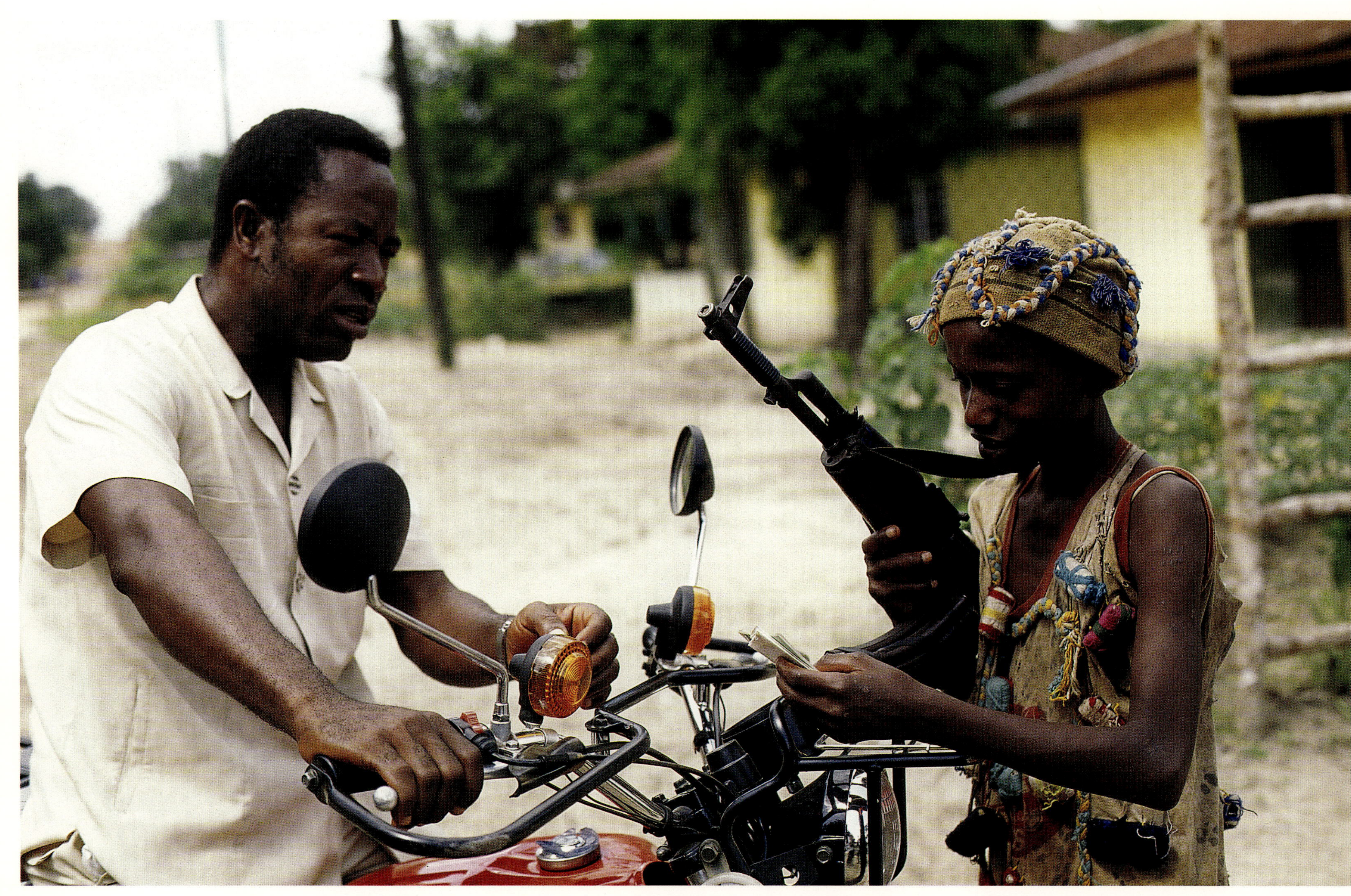

A child soldier checks for passes at a road block. Photograph by Giacomo Pirozzi/Panos

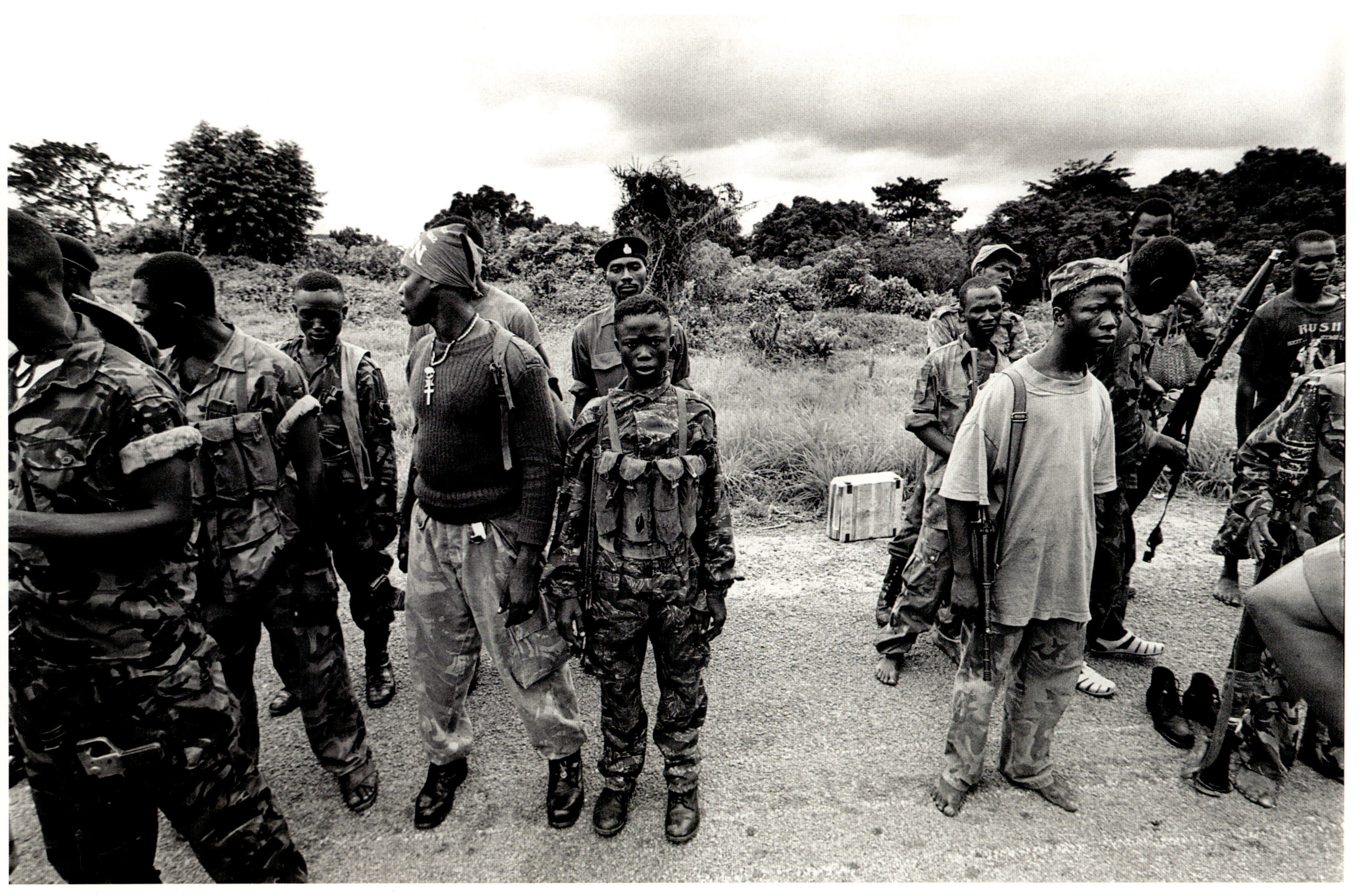

A child soldier stands with others in Sierra Leone. Photograph by Kadir van Lohuizen/Noor

africa: sudan

An armed child with Janjaweed fighters.
Photograph by Lynsey Addario

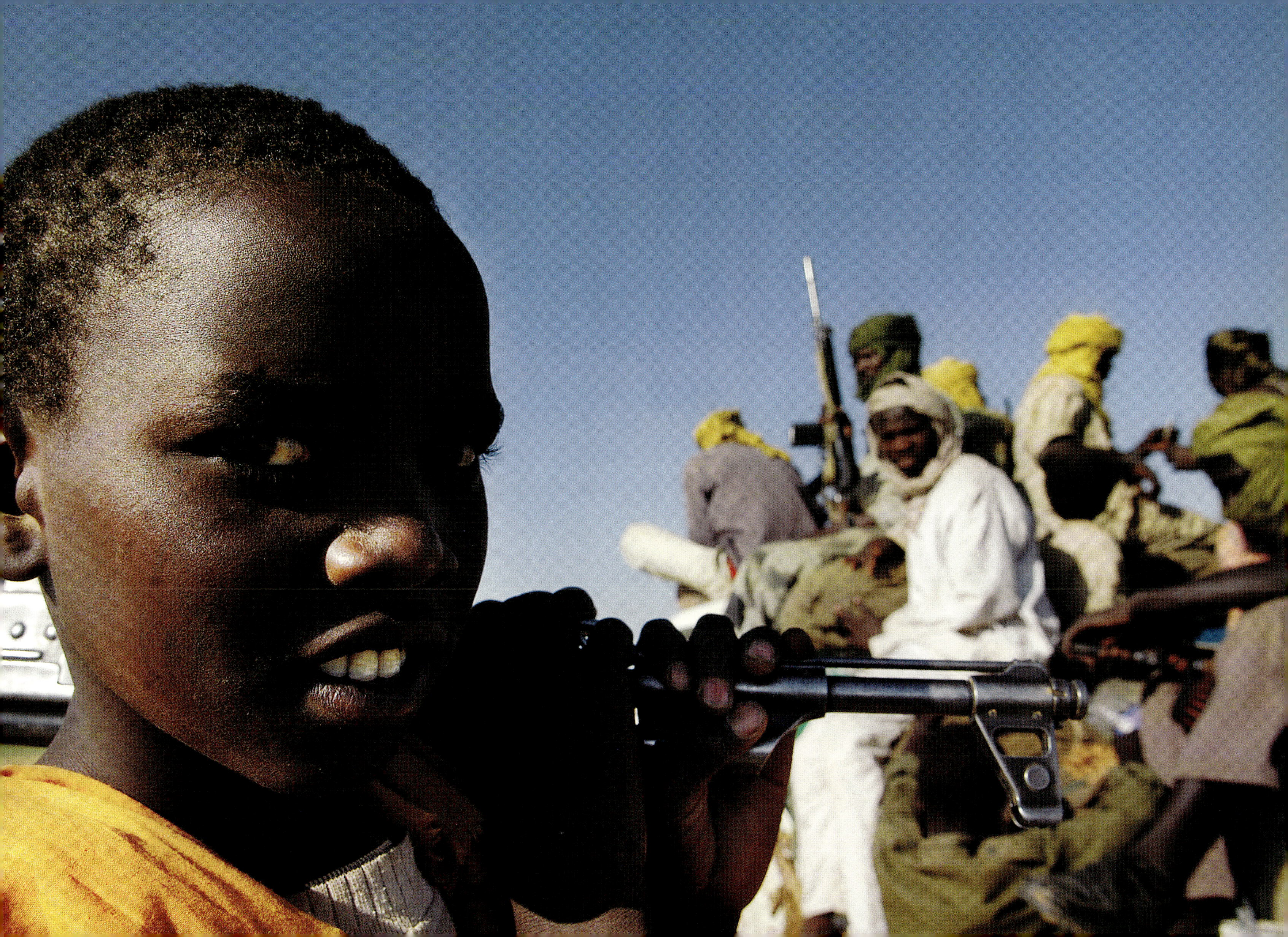

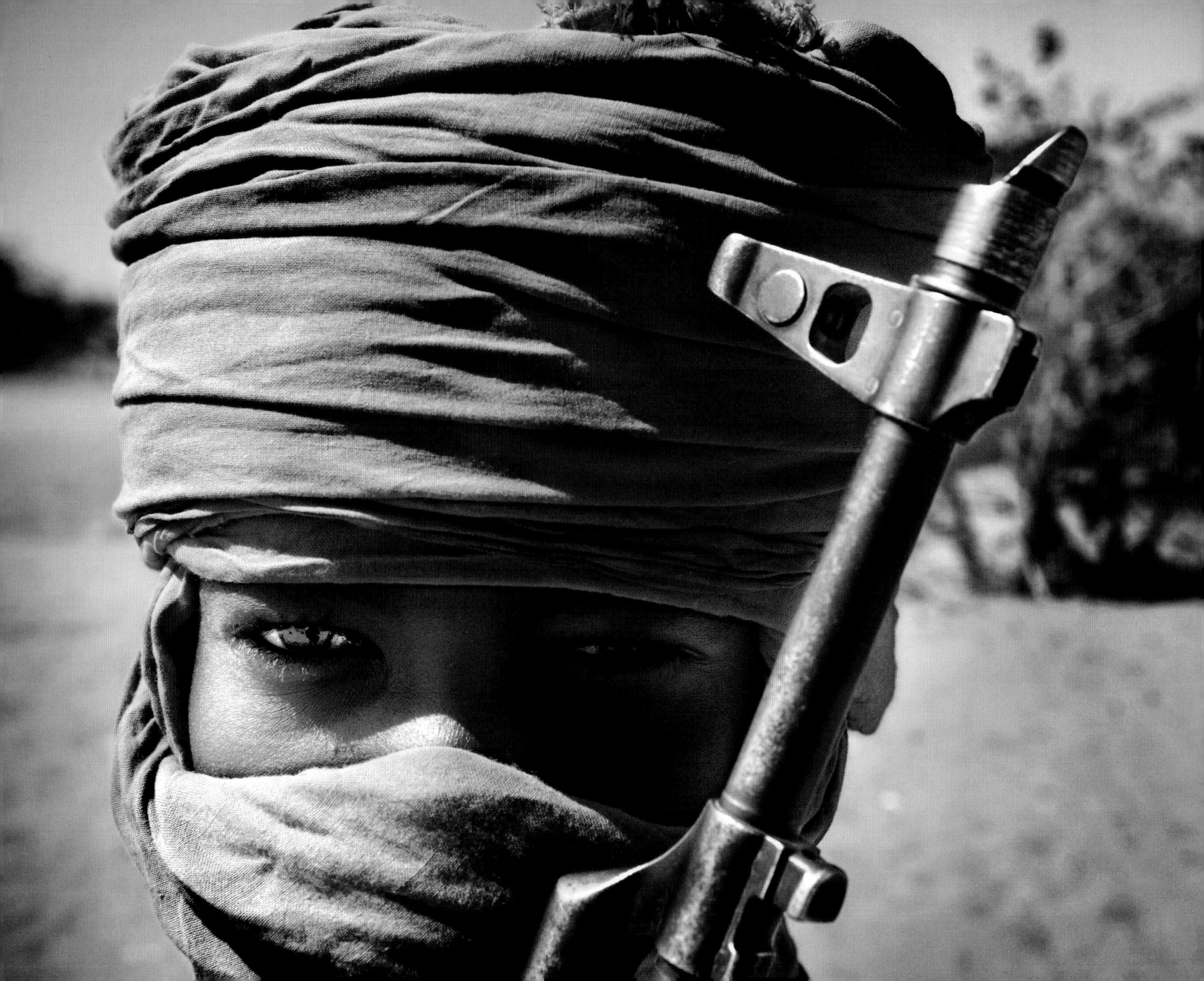

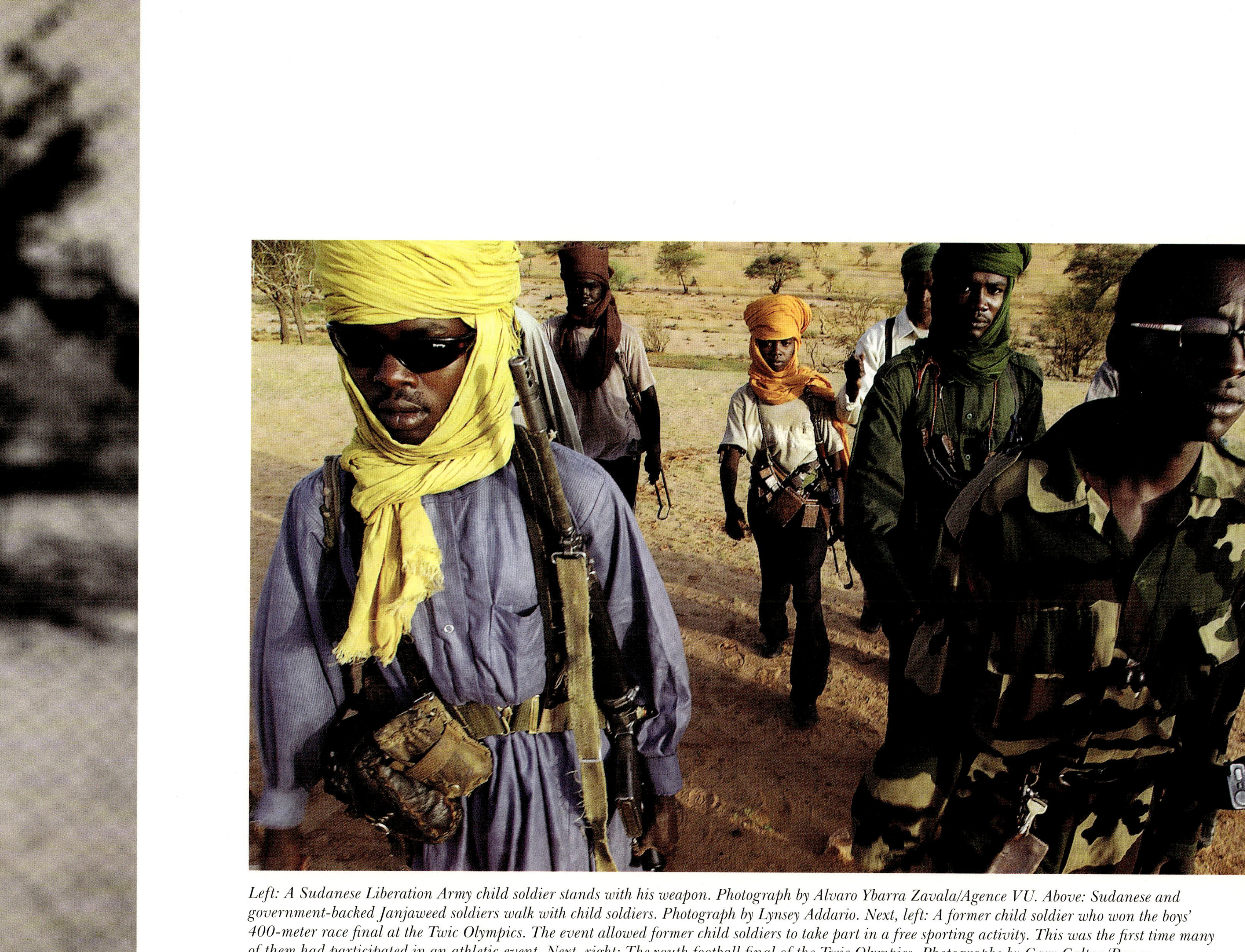

Left: A Sudanese Liberation Army child soldier stands with his weapon. Photograph by Alvaro Ybarra Zavala/Agence VU. Above: Sudanese and government-backed Janjaweed soldiers walk with child soldiers. Photograph by Lynsey Addario. Next, left: A former child soldier who won the boys' 400-meter race final at the Twic Olympics. The event allowed former child soldiers to take part in a free sporting activity. This was the first time many of them had participated in an athletic event. Next, right: The youth football final of the Twic Olympics. Photographs by Gary Calton/Panos

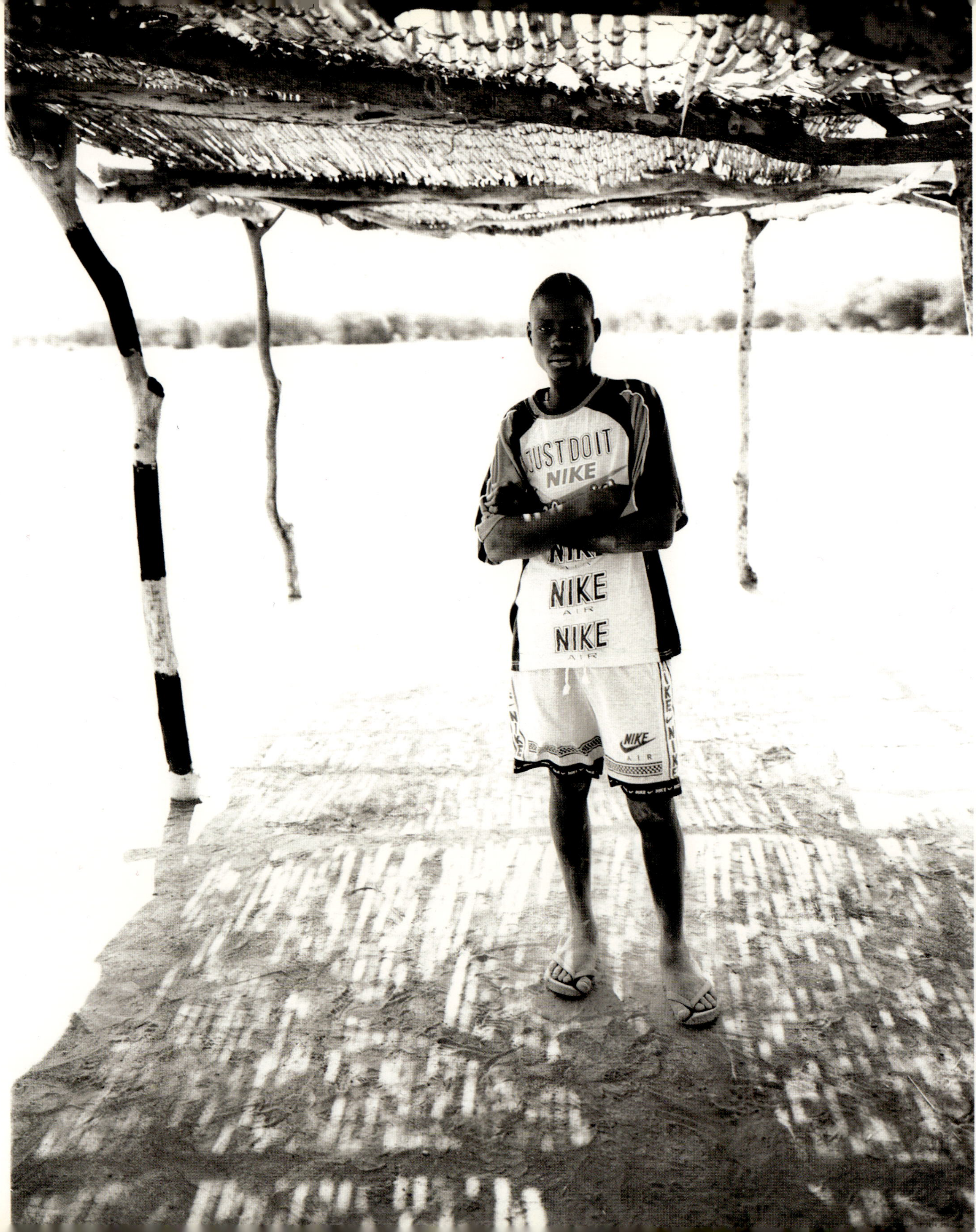

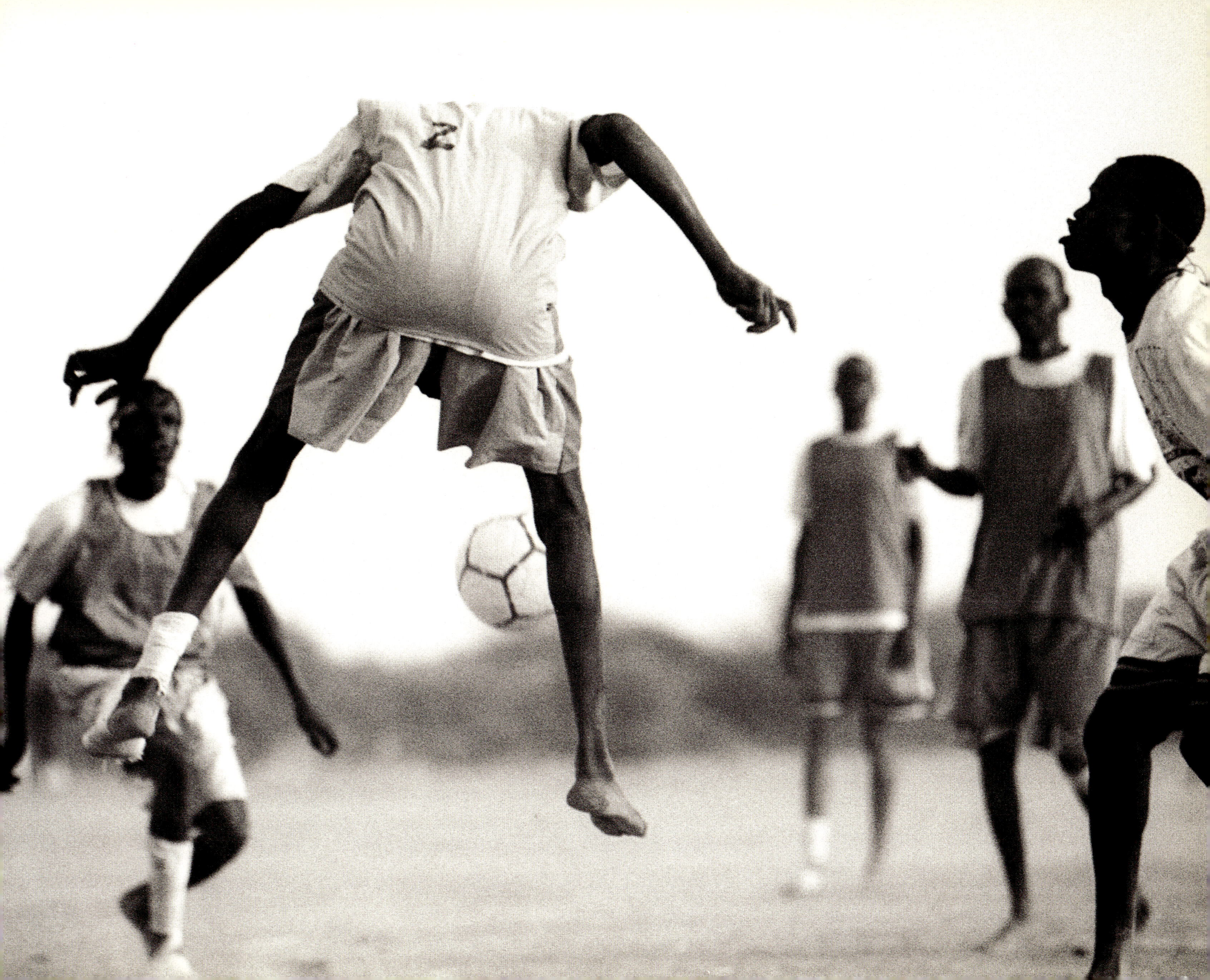

Desperation, Deprivation, Exploitation

Jo Becker

Sakuntala joined the Tamil Tigers in Sri Lanka when she was 15. The rebels had already visited her home numerous times, demanding that her parents give a son or a daughter for "the cause." Finally Sakuntala agreed to go, afraid that if she refused, the rebels would take her younger sister instead.

Aung was only 11 when a recruiter threatened him with jail if he refused to join Burma's national army. He was beaten during training and sent into combat for the first time when he was only 12. "I was terrified," he said. "I shot my gun into the air, because I was afraid if I didn't shoot, my commander would punish me."

Peter was seven and living on the streets when he joined a Colombian guerilla group. His father was dead and his mother was very poor. "I went hungry most of the time," he said. "I thought that if I left home, my mother and my brothers would be fewer and would eat better."

Every child soldier's story is unique. Some are abducted or forcibly recruited. Others—their lives devastated by poverty or war—join out of desperation. As society breaks down during conflict, children are left with no access to school, and are often driven from their homes or separated from their families. Many perceive armed groups as their best chance for survival—or simply a guarantee of at least one meal per day.

Some children join because they want to be part of a cause and believe they are fighting for their people. Others want revenge because of atrocities perpetrated against their families or communities. And some are motivated by the status or the lure of a uniform, a gun, or a promised salary.

Regardless of how they become soldiers, these children share the common experience of gross exploitation by commanders eager for young, malleable recruits, and too often, a life of brutality, deprivation, and violence.

Today, children under the age of 18 are being used as soldiers in government armies, rebel forces, and pro-government paramilitaries in nearly 20 countries worldwide. Most are adolescents, though some are as young as seven.

Some armed groups simply would not exist if not for child soldiers. In Northern Uganda, for example, the Lord's Resistance Army (LRA) alienated the civilian population with its brutal tactics. Unable to find willing adult volunteers, it has abducted over 25,000 children into its ranks over the past two decades. It is believed that over 85 percent of LRA soldiers were abducted as children.

Many commanders target children for their forces because they believe children are more easily indoctrinated and follow orders more easily, particularly if they do not understand the consequences of what they are being asked to do. A former child soldier in Colombia told Human Rights Watch, "The commanders prefer minors because they learn better.... The ideal recruit is about 13, because then they can get a full political education."

Some groups use indoctrination as a way of recruiting children. Prior to the 2006 cease-fire in Nepal, Maoist forces often visited rural schools to present cultural programs that included singing, dancing, and speeches. The Maoists would tell the children that they were fighting for the people, fighting against corruption, and that everyone needed to support them. One 16-year-old boy told Human Rights Watch that the Maoists started coming to his school when he was in grade six, and came nearly every day for three years. By the time he was in grade nine, he said that out of his 50 classmates, 45 had already joined the Maoists. He said, "I decided to join too. I was very impressed with their speeches and influenced by what they said about fighting for the people."

Compared to adult soldiers, who may have more training and experience, children are often considered expendable. As a result, they are often favored for particularly dangerous duties. They may be used as cannon fodder, sent into battle ahead of adult troops, or used as human mine detectors. In battles in the Democratic Republic of Congo, children have been deliberately pushed into battle armed only with sticks, and ordered to beat their sticks against trees to draw fire from the enemy. While the children create a diversion, older troops mount an offensive from another direction. Not surprisingly, many children have been slaughtered in this way.

While the typical perception of a child soldier is often an African boy armed with an AK-47, a significant number of child soldiers are girls. In many conflicts, such as those in Uganda, Colombia, Sri Lanka, and the Democratic Republic of Congo, over 30 percent of child soldiers are girls. One study found that girls were active fighters in 34 conflicts between the years 1990 and 2003.

Girls serve in all of the same capacities as boys, often bearing arms and fighting in combat. In Sri Lanka, the Tamil Tigers have often used young girls as suicide bombers, believing they are less likely to arouse suspicion at military checkpoints. In many conflicts, girls are also sexually exploited. In Northern Uganda, girls abducted by the LRA are commonly forced to become "wives" to LRA commanders and are subjected to repeated rapes, exposure to sexually transmitted diseases, and unwanted pregnancies. According to some estimates, more than 3,000 babies have been born to girls who have been sexually enslaved by the LRA.

In Sierra Leone, where an estimated 12,000 child soldiers during the civil war were girls, one study found that all of the girls who said their primary role was a "fighter" were also forced to be wives. Some girls were sent into battle during their seventh month of pregnancy.

As wars end and peace agreements are reached, tens of thousands of children have been demobilized from fighting forces in countries like Sierra Leone, Liberia, Burundi, and the Democratic Republic of Congo. In ongoing conflicts, children sometimes manage to run away from their commanders, are captured, or are otherwise released. But even after leaving armed forces and groups, these children often face tough challenges rejoining civilian society. Many have been out of school for years, and have no civilian job skills. Some have lost their families, and are on their own. Girls who have been sexually exploited may have to worry about supporting not only themselves, but also their babies.

At the international level, a range of efforts are confronting the recruitment and use of child soldiers. A UN treaty adopted in 2000 sets 18 as the minimum age to participation in armed conflict or for any compulsory recruitment. Since its adoption, 120 governments have ratified the treaty. Some, like the United States, have changed their deployment or recruitment practices as a result.

These efforts have yielded some progress. But impunity remains a big problem. Many commanders continue to recruit and use child soldiers because they believe—too often correctly— that they will face no negative consequences for their crime. That has to change. Only with strong and consistent action by the international community will commanders realize that they cannot recruit children without being held accountable.

Jo Becker is the Children's Rights Advocacy Director for Human Rights Watch and the founding chairperson of the Coalition to Stop the Use of Child Soldiers.

middle east: palestine and iraq

A young Palestinian boy throws tear gas back at Israeli soldiers. Photograph by Colin Finlay

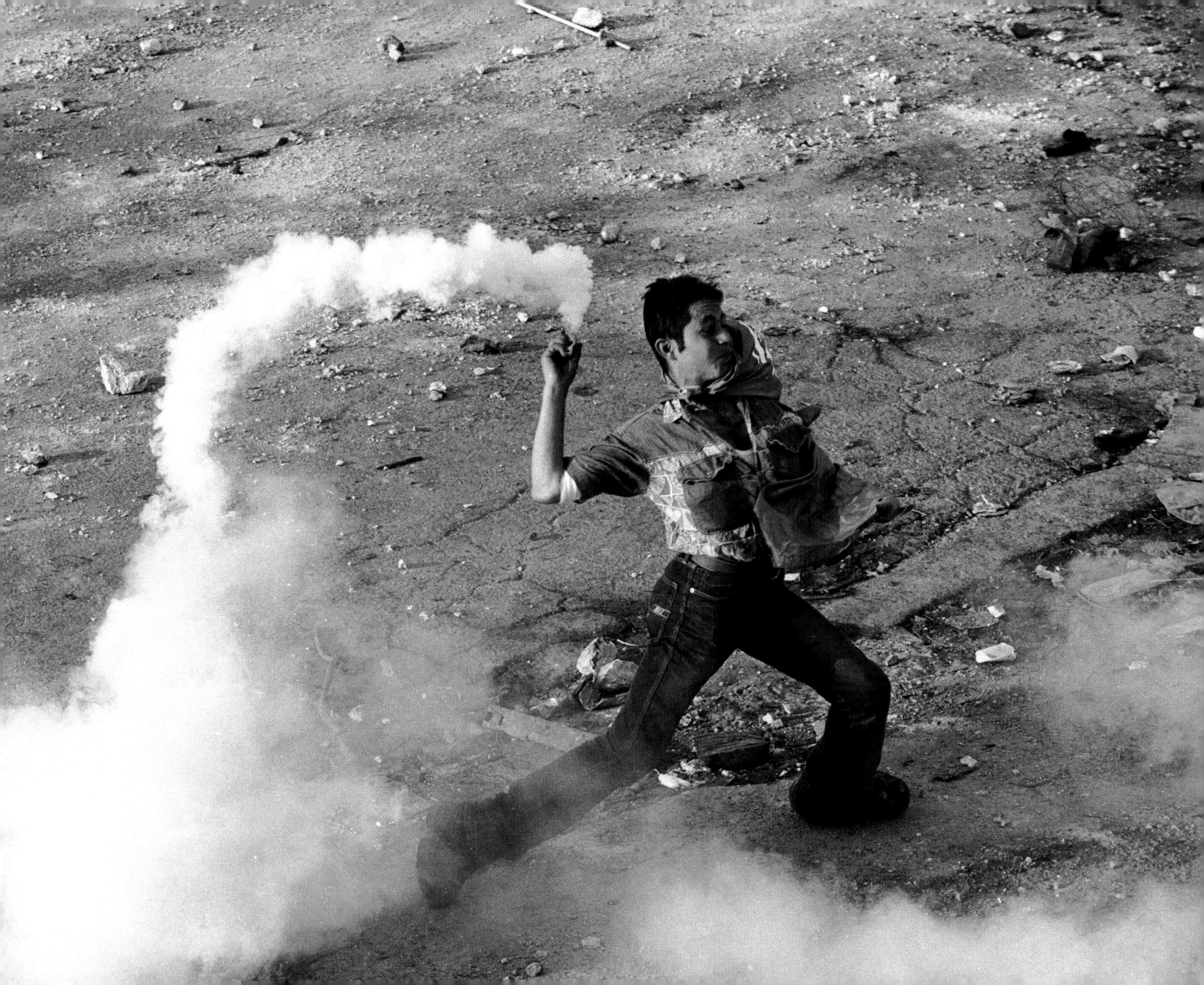

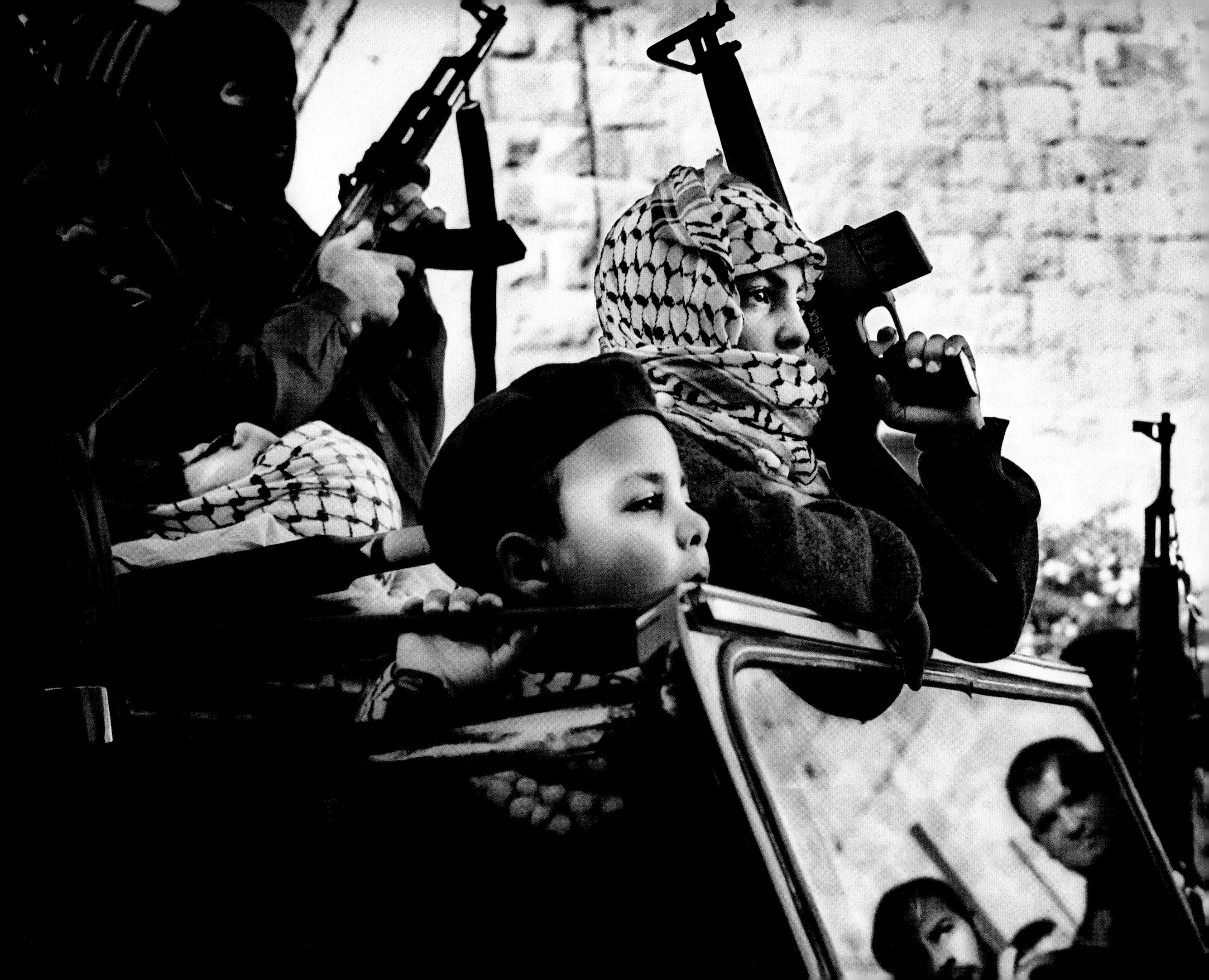
PULL BACK

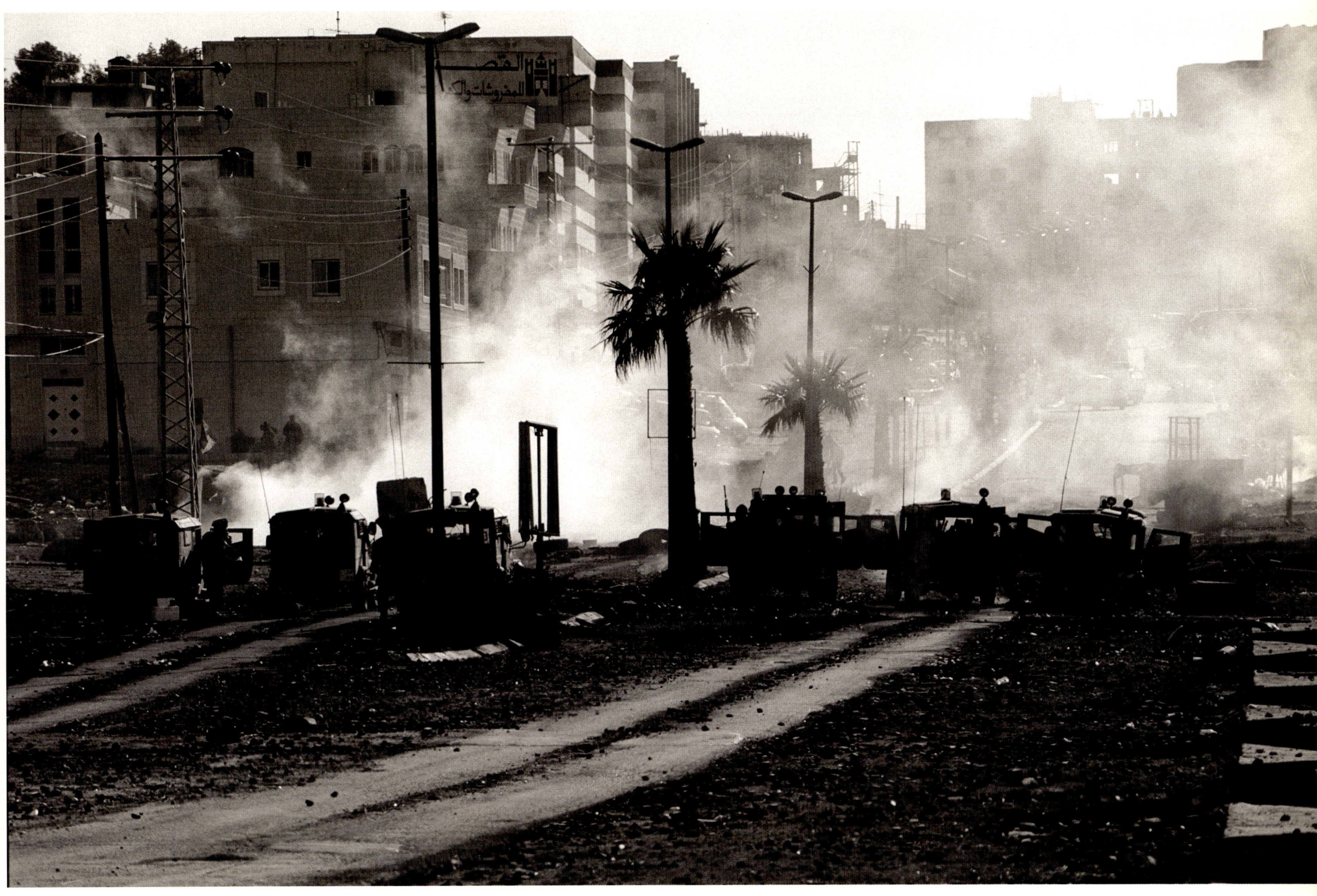

Left: Young Fatah members at the funeral of a Palestinian fighter. Photograph by Jan Grarup/Noor. Above: Israeli Defense Forces in Ramallah. Photograph by Colin Finlay

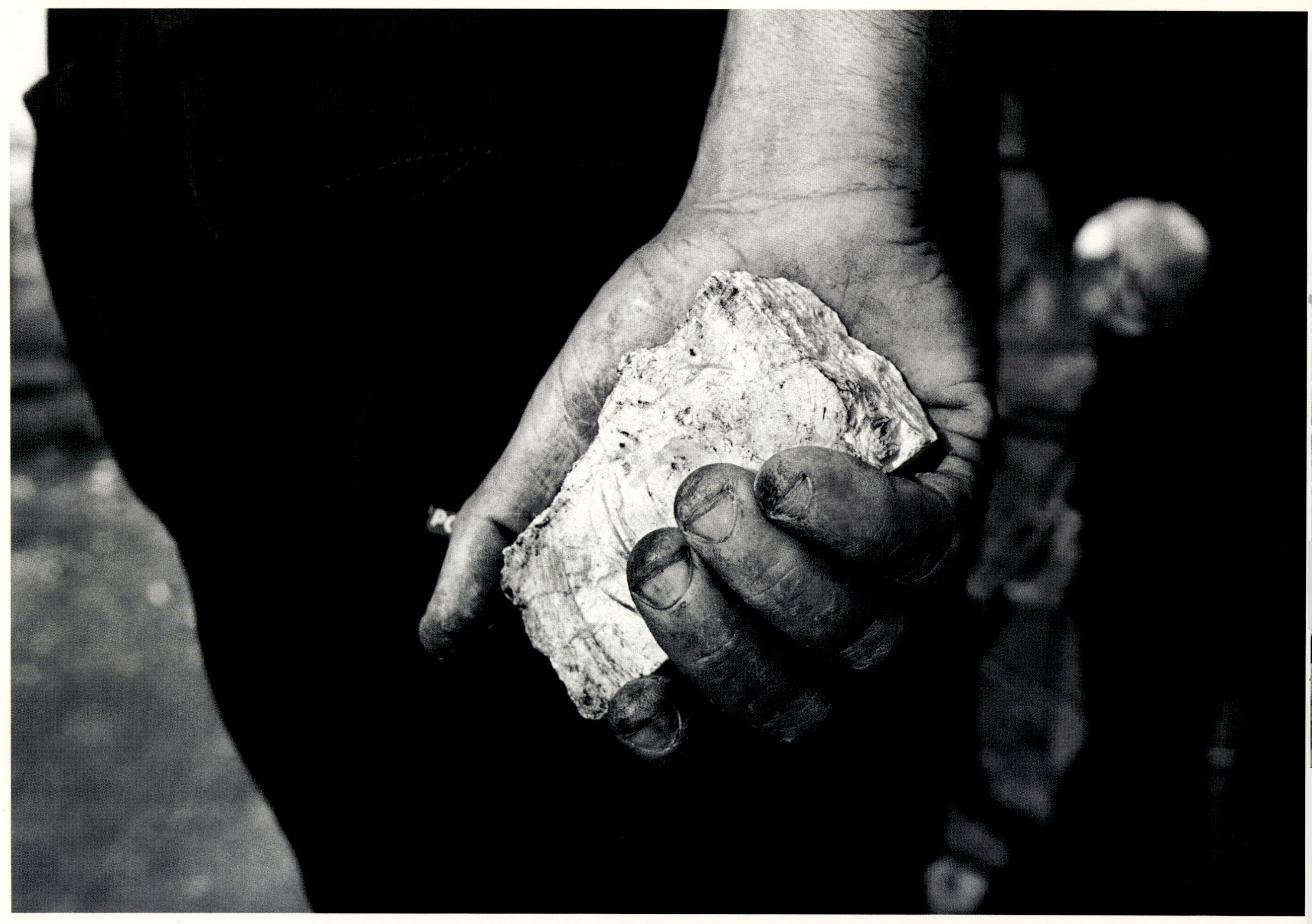

Above: Boy in Ramallah. Photograph by Colin Finlay. Right: In Ramallah, young boys train with Tanzim, the militant wing of Fatah. Photograph by Jan Grarup/Noor

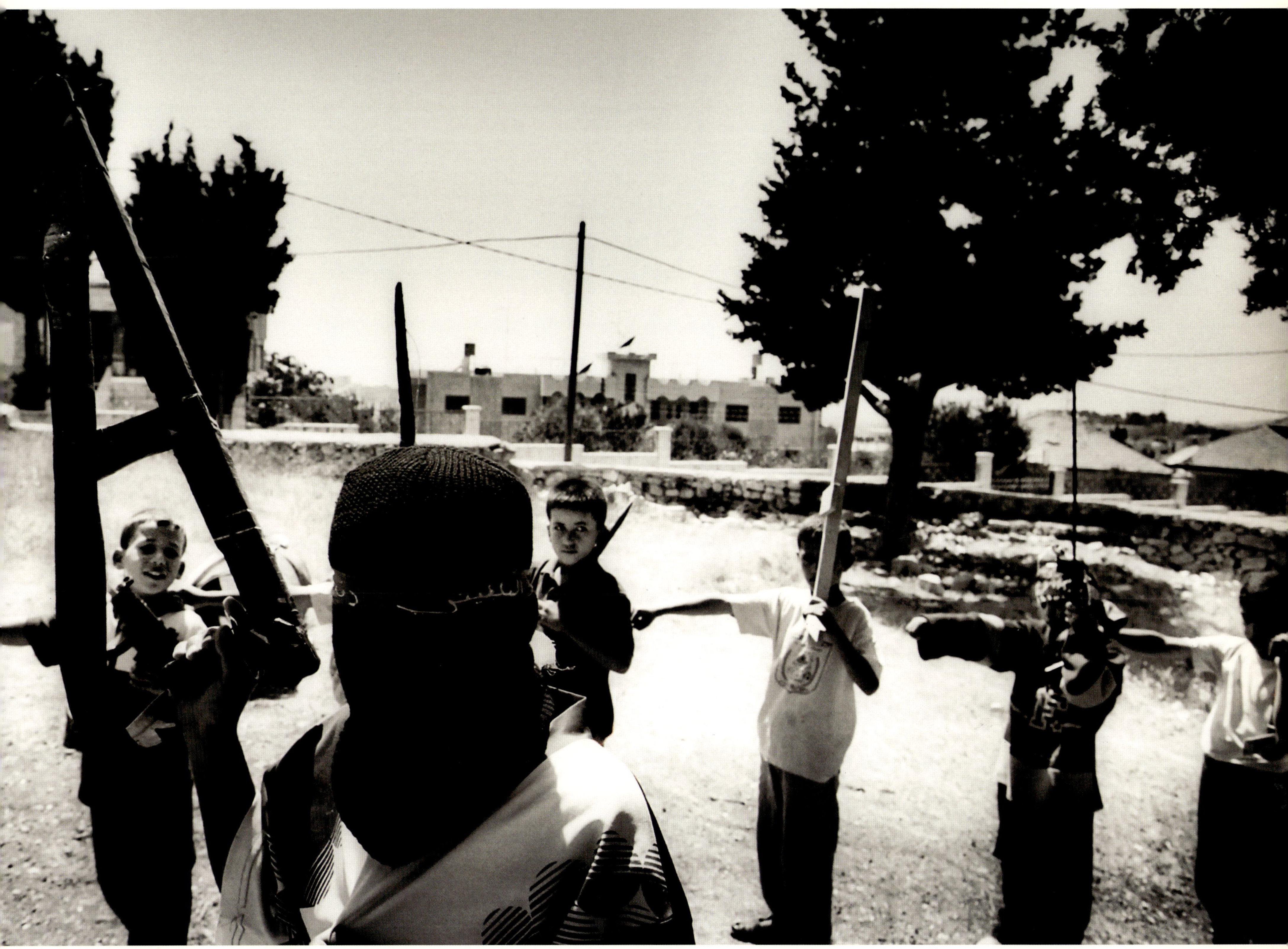

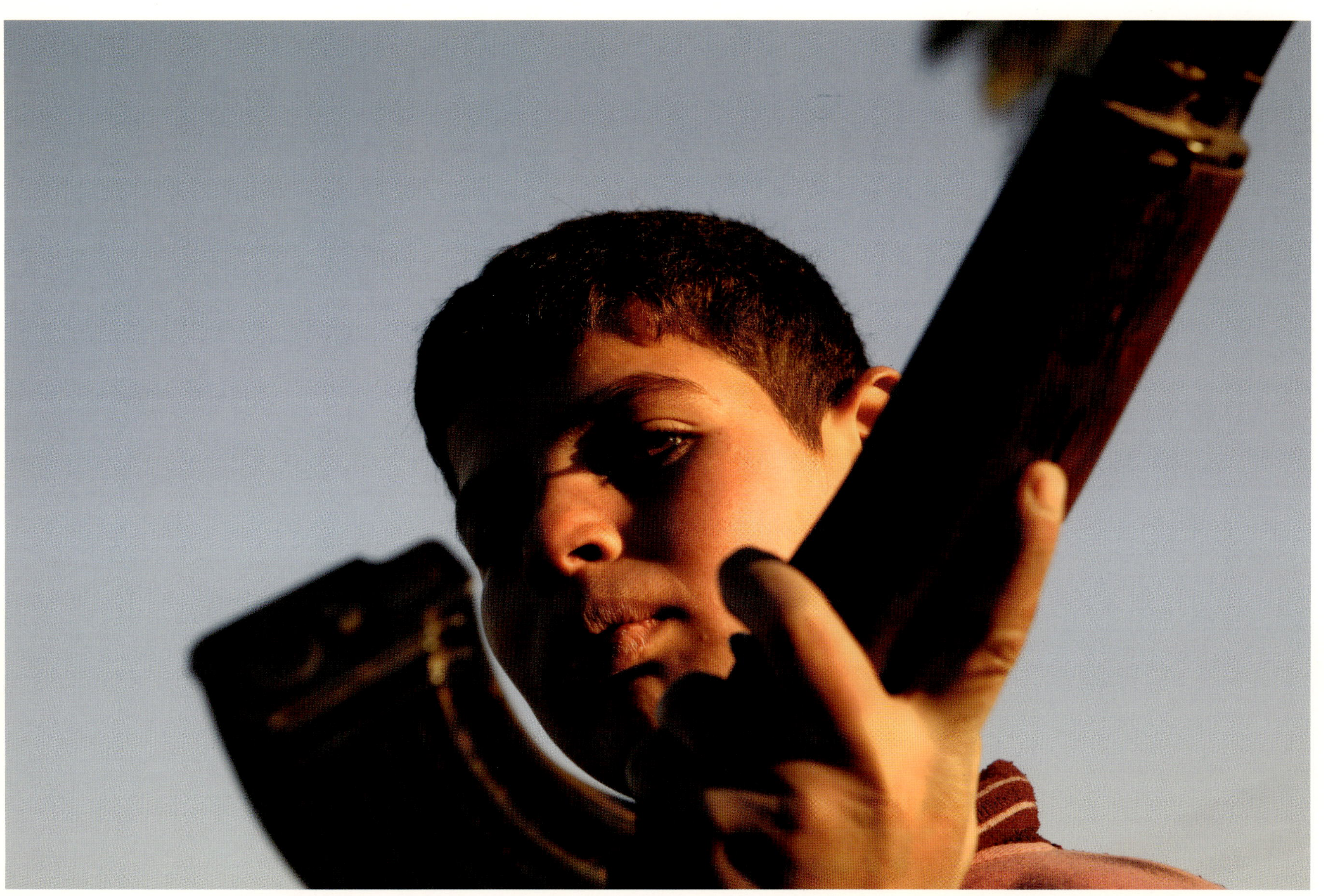

Militia boys holding Kalashnikov rifles at a checkpoint in Baghdad. Photographs by Gaith Abdul-Ahad/Getty Images

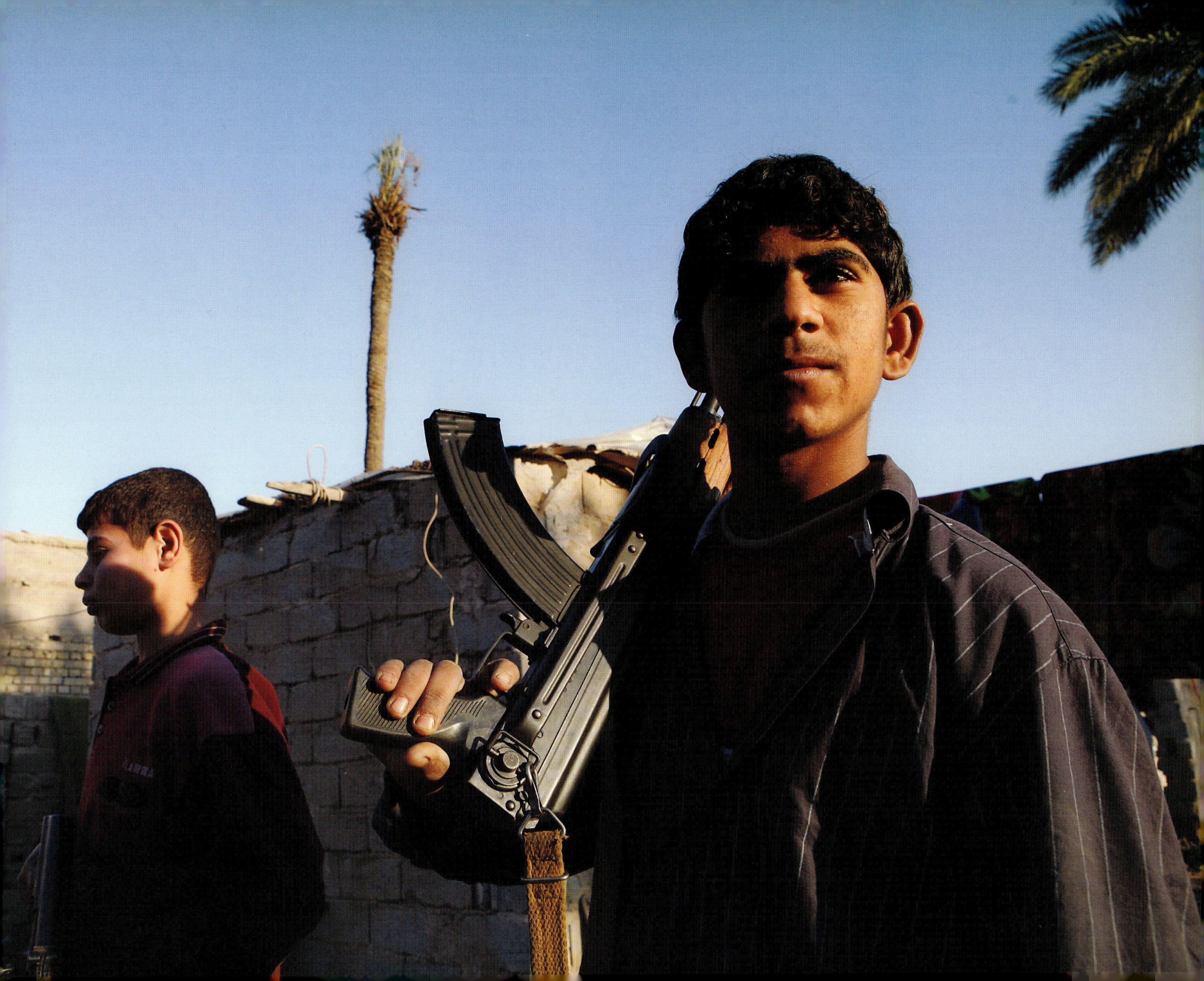

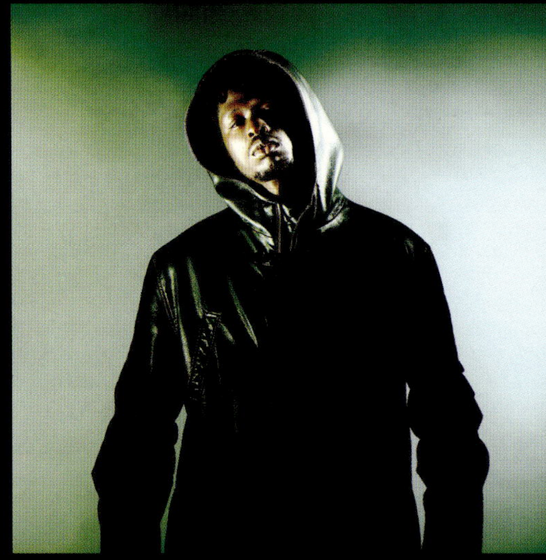

I believe I have survived for a reason
To tell my story, to touch lives

All people struggling down there
Storms only come for a while
Then after a while they'll be gone
Bless, bless

My father was working for the government as a policeman
A few years later I heard he joined a rebel movement
That was formed to fight for freedom
I didn't understand the politics behind all this
Coz I was only a child
After a while I saw the tension rising high
Between the Christian and the Muslim regimes
We lost our possessions
My mother, my mother's mother suffered depression
And because of this I was forced to be a warchild

Chorus:
I'm a warchild
Ana gi kore korea, ana gi kore korea, kore korea, kore korea

I believe I have survived for a reason
To tell my story, to touch lives

I lost my father and mother in this battle
My brothers too perished in this struggle
All my life I've been hiding in the jungle
The pain I'm carrying is too much to handle
Who's there please to light up my candle?
Is there anyone to hear my cry?
Here I am pale and dry

Mbwona leaders wanna wonder why
Na watototo Kule wanna die
Hakuna Mutu mwenye wanna care
Our shame is everywhere
In our pain watu wanna gain
Wanna pray to maintain
Wanna pray tu to maintain

Chorus

Emmanuel Jal was born in war-torn Sudan in the early 1980s. He was taken from his family home in 1987 when he was six or seven years old, and sent to fight with the rebel army in Sudan's bloody civil war. For nearly five years, he was a "child warrior," put into battle carrying an AK-47 that was taller than he was. By the time he was 13, he was a veteran of two civil wars and had seen hundreds of his fellow child soldiers reduced to taking unspeakable measures as they struggled to survive on the killing fields of southern Sudan. After a series of harrowing events, a British aid worker smuggled him into Nairobi to raise him as her own. To help ease the pain of what he had experienced, Emmanuel started singing. In 2005, he released his first album, *Gua* ("peace" in his native Nuer tongue), with the title track broadcast across Africa over the BBC and becoming a number one hit in Kenya. *Gua* also earned him a spot at Bob Geldof's "Live 8" concert in the UK. He frequently speaks on college campus about his experiences, in an effort to raise awareness of and halt the inhumane treatment of children in Sudan

Hope for the Integration of Formerly Recruited Children

Mike Wessells

"Born Killers"..."Lost Generation"..."No Hope for Rehabilitation"...

These are the kinds of headlines and lead-ins to radio shows heard from war zones around the world in regard to former child soldiers. They are sensational and they sell. The question is, are they true?

Fifteen-year-old Mirwais had fought for the Northern Alliance. He fought because "I wanted to help my family and my people." To him, the Taliban were oppressors who aimed to impose an extreme form of religion and government on his community. When his father, uncle, and brother joined up with the local commander, Mirwais also joined.

When the war was over, Mirwais wanted to go to school. The war had destroyed most schools and most boys had to work to help their families survive. Fortunately, ChildFund Afghanistan organized youth groups and literacy classes that Mirwais took part in. Upon demonstrating that he could sign his name, he beamed proudly saying, "Now I can do business and not be ashamed." Mirwais also worked after school at the local market, helping to feed his family. His integration into civilian life went well because his family members also returned to civilian life. Others respected him as he had the education and livelihood expected of a young Afghan man. He had never seen himself as a natural killer, only as a soldier who had followed orders and done what he had been trained to do. His respect for the sanctity of life had remained intact.

Joyce had been abducted at 16 by the rebels in rural Sierra Leone and was told she must fight or die. Reluctant at first, she observed that those who carried weapons and fought commanded greater respect than those who served as porters, cooks, or "soldiers' wives" (more appropriately called "sex slaves"). She welcomed the idea of having a gun because "I didn't want to be one of girls who gets raped." Joyce became known as a fierce fighter. She said "no one touched me because they knew I would get them if they tried." She had regularly abused drugs such as alcohol and marijuana as a soldier and had "gotten used to that way of life."

Initially, Joyce didn't seem a likely candidate for integration into civilian life. Following the war, at age 20, Joyce went back to her village. People humiliated her, taunting her as a "rebel girl." Upset, she fled to Freetown in search of a job. There her aunt helped her remember the importance of good behavior. A good communicator and organizer, Joyce found a job six months later with an international NGO that taught former girl recruits

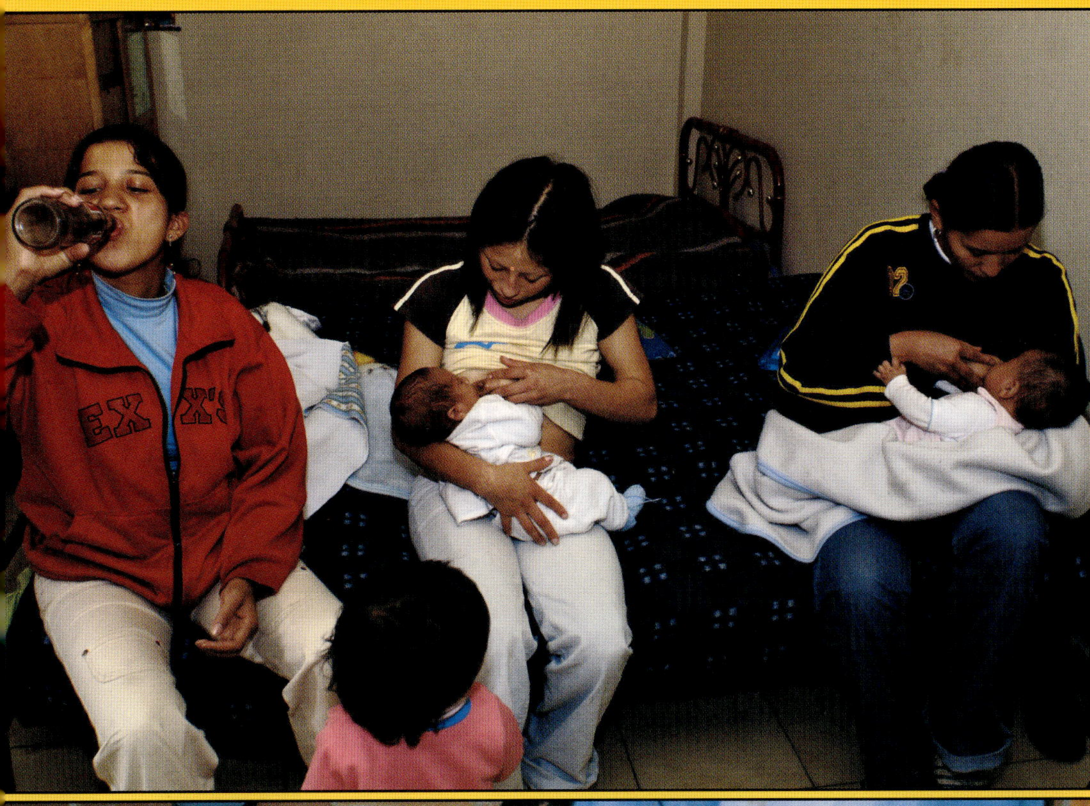

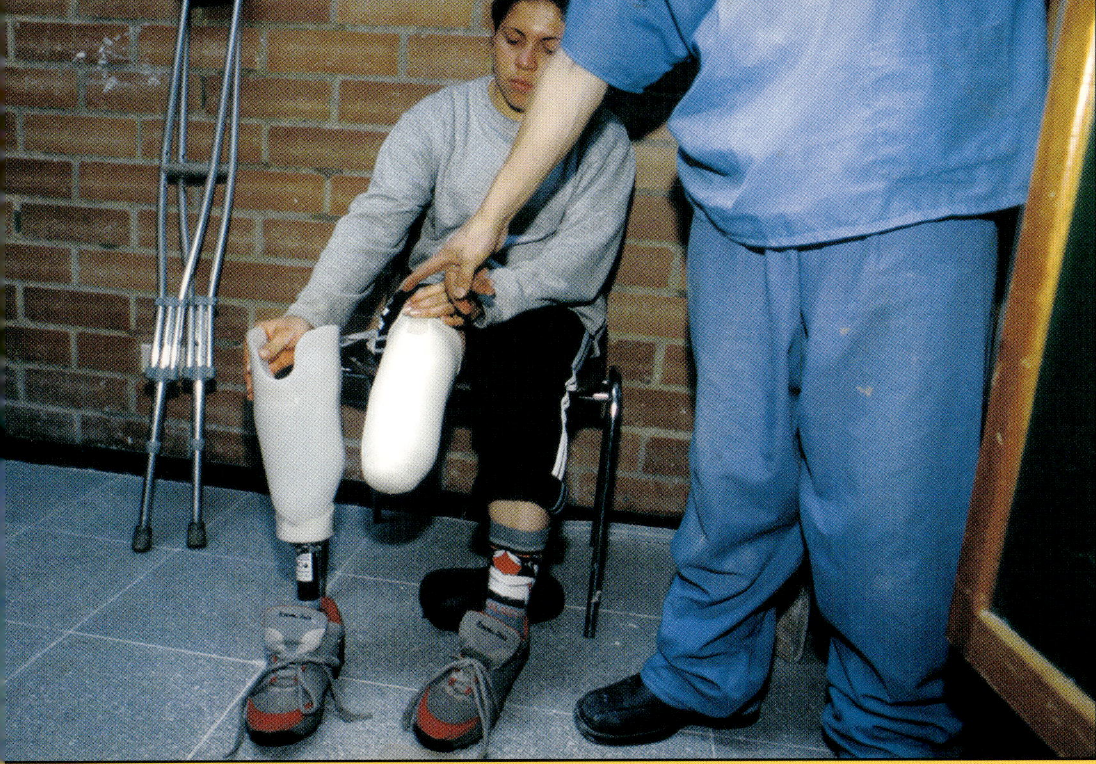

"Born Killers"..."Lost Generation"..."No Hope for Rehabilitation"...

These are the kinds of headlines and lead-ins to radio shows heard from war zones around the world in regard to former child soldiers. They are sensational and they sell. The question is, are they true?

Fifteen-year-old Mirwais had fought for the Northern Alliance. He fought because "I wanted to help my family and my people." To him, the Taliban were oppressors who aimed to impose an extreme form of religion and government on his community. When his father, uncle, and brother joined up with the local commander, Mirwais also joined.

When the war was over, Mirwais wanted to go to school. The war had destroyed most schools and most boys had to work to help their families survive. Fortunately, ChildFund Afghanistan organized youth groups and literacy classes that Mirwais took part in. Upon demonstrating that he could sign his name, he beamed proudly saying, "Now I can do business and not be ashamed." Mirwais also worked after school at the local market, helping to feed his family. His integration into civilian life went well because his family members also returned to civilian life. Others respected him as he had the education and livelihood expected of a young Afghan man. He had never seen himself as a natural killer, only as a soldier who had followed orders and done what he had been trained to do. His respect for the sanctity of life had remained intact.

Photographs by Donna De Cesare

such as international aid agencies. These are some of the main kinds of support that have proven useful in different countries:

Community mobilization and reconciliation. Because communities often fear, retaliate against, or stigmatize returning child soldiers, it is important to build empathy with formerly recruited children. Through community discussions everyone learns about the suffering of all young people, including those who had been recruited. Traditional reconciliation activities may involve singing, dancing, or the conduct of rituals. Engaging returning children in community service projects enables community members to see the young people not as troublemakers and warriors but as contributing members of society.

Family tracing, integration, and mediation. Since many recruited children have been torn from their families, a vital step is to locate their families and reunite them. Supportive discussions by trained outsiders with family members help families to handle the conflicts that may erupt between a returning child and siblings or parents.

Education. Many returning children are in the process of redefining their social identity away from soldiering and toward civilian life. To accomplish this identity shift and have hope for the future, children need to have education. Field experience has shown that non-formal education, catch-up classes, and literacy courses can be very useful when going to school is not an option.

Livelihoods. When children exit armed groups, one of their greatest concerns is how they will feed themselves and earn a living. This concern is not only about money but also about finding an appropriate place in the civilian world. Useful supports include training in locally marketable skills and making small loans that enable them to start their own businesses. As these young people work in appropriate civilian ways, local people come to see them in a new light. In turn, this change enables the children to remake their identities as civilians.

Psychosocial support. Following horrific experiences inside armed groups, young people need psychosocial support. Mentoring and peer group discussions, and in some cases, counseling for severely affected youth, all are helpful with the reintegration into society.

Sometimes, spiritual supports are greatly needed. A boy in Angola who had killed a man in combat and experienced nightmares characteristic of post-traumatic stress disorder, said, "I cannot sleep at night because the man I killed…his spirit comes to me at night and asks 'Why did you do this to me?'" An angry spirit haunted this boy. According to local customs the spirit could harm not only the boy but also his family and village. A local healer conducted a ritual of purification that "cleansed" the boy, putting his mind at ease and enabling the villagers to accept him as a civilian.

Health care. Recruited children face health issues associated not only with attacks and landmines but also with issues such as malnutrition. Girls often face a complex array of reproductive health issues, including sexually

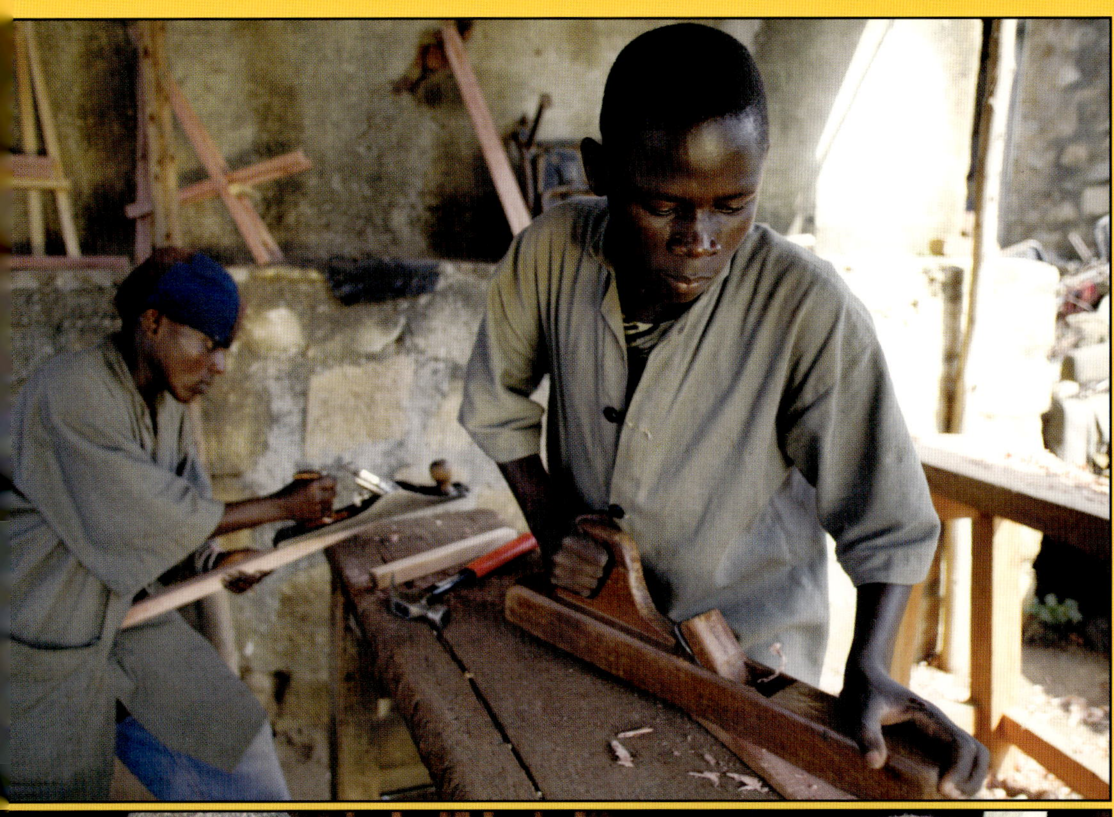

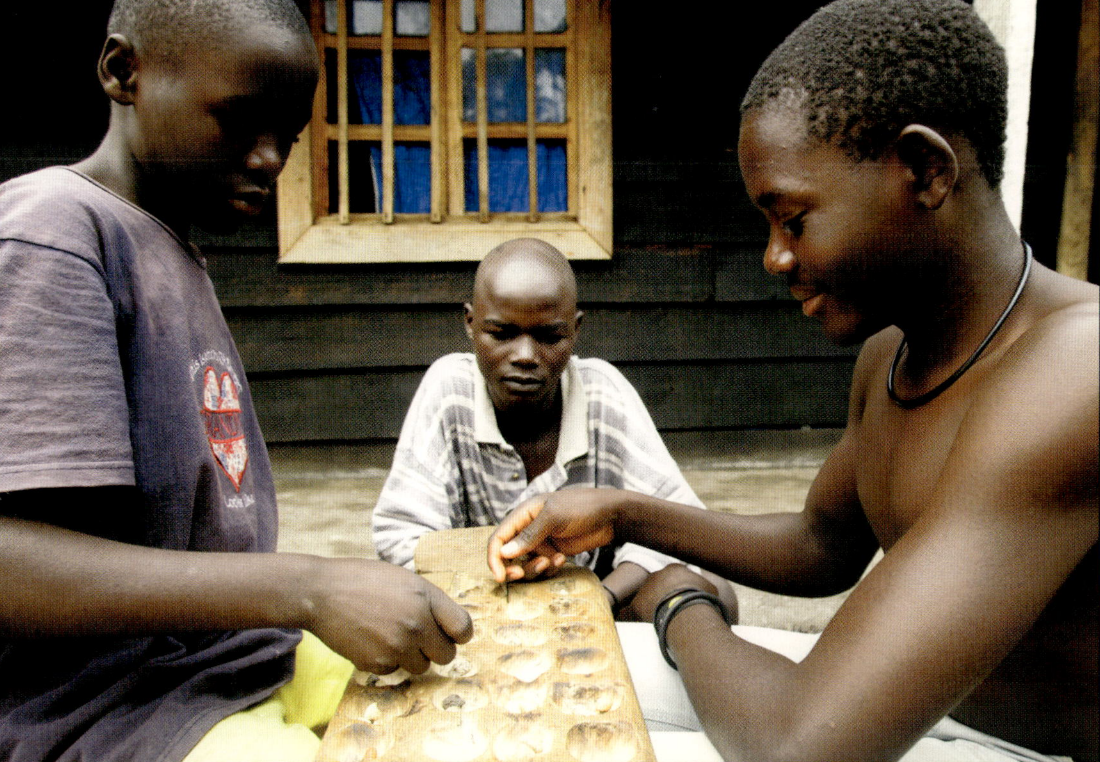

transmitted infections that add to the stigma and agony that they and their children suffer. Access to health care is fundamental for integration and well-being.

Protection. Because re-recruitment is often an ongoing threat in war zones, it is essential to organize systems of protection that prevent re-recruitment and other risks that can harm children, such as gender-based violence, trafficking, and living on the streets. These systems ought to provide ongoing monitoring, reporting, and action by communities, governments, civil society leaders, and international agencies.

Often harm is caused unintentionally by singling recruited children out by giving them benefits such as cash and tools that are denied to other war-affected children. This divides the community and stigmatizes former child recruits at the moment when the need is greatest for social unity and support. A better approach is to make support of the former recruits part of a package for all war-affected children in the community. Participation is a child's right, and having a voice in one's destiny is part of the process of rebuilding hope.

Mike Wessells is Senior Advisor on Child Protection for Christian Children's Fund and Professor of Clinical Population and Family Health at Colombia University.

Top: Ex-child combatants receive carpentry skills training at a UNICEF-funded rehabilitation center. Bottom: Former child soldiers play a game of Bao at a rehabilitation center. Photographs by Giacomo Pirozzi/Panos

Conflict Countries

AFGHANISTAN
In 2003, there were an estimated 8,000 former child soldiers in Afghanistan. Many of them have left the fighting forces voluntarily, but still need support and assistance to reintegrate into civilian life. Some have served in the army as non-combatants, working as cooks, porters, guards, or messengers. (UNICEF)

BURMA
Burma is believed to have more child soldiers than any other country in the world. The overwhelming majority of Burma's child soldiers are found in Burma's national army, the Tatmadaw Kyi, which forcibly recruits children as young as 11, subjects them to brutal training, and forces them to engage in combat and participate in human rights abuses against civilians. Children are also present in Burma's myriad opposition groups, although in far smaller numbers. (Human Rights Watch)

COLOMBIA
More than 11,000 children fight in Colombia's armed conflict, one of the highest totals in the world. Both guerrilla and paramilitary forces rely on child combatants, who have been forced to commit atrocities and execute other children who try to desert. Colombia's illegal armies have recruited increasing numbers of children in recent years. (Human Rights Watch)

DEMOCRATIC REPUBLIC OF CONGO
DRC is at the top of the list of countries where armed forces and militia groups use children as soldiers, sex slaves, or laborers. There may be as many as 30,000 Congolese children fighting or living with armed forces or militia groups; an estimated 30 to 40 percent of them are girls. Children are forced into service, and many are left with no choice but to join the militias, which may offer some protection and provisions. (UNICEF)

IRAQ
Iraqi law has perpetuated the use of children as soldiers. Children are believed to have been used during the 1991 Gulf War. In 2002, 1,000 children were believed to be in the official Iraqi government armed forces. There are indications of children being recruited as combatants and as decoys in suicide car bombings by non-state armed groups, such as insurgency organizations. (UN Office of Children and Armed Conflict)

LIBERIA
More than 15,000 child soldiers made up many of the fighting units on all sides of the Liberian civil war. In August 2003, a comprehensive peace agreement ended 14 years of conflict. (Human Rights Watch)

NEPAL
Thousands of children were recruited by the Communist Party of Nepal (Maoists) during Nepal's 10-year civil war, and carried out crucial military and logistical support duties. Even after signing a comprehensive peace agreement with the government in November 2006, the Maoists continued to recruit children and refused to release them from their forces. (Human Rights Watch)

OCCUPIED WEST BANK AND GAZA STRIP/ PALESTINIAN AUTHORITY TERRITORIES
Human Rights Watch has documented several cases of children carrying out suicide bombings.

SIERRA LEONE
Between February and June 1998, both the government's Civil Defense Forces (CDF) and the ousted Armed Forces Revolutionary Council (AFRC) as well as the Revolutionary United Front (RUF) continued to use children on a large scale in Sierra Leone. (Human Rights Watch)

SRI LANKA
The Karuna group has abducted hundreds of children in eastern Sri Lanka for use as child combatants since 1987. The group is led by a former commander of the Liberation Tigers of Tamil Eelam (LTTE) and now fights against the LTTE. Government security forces not only fail to stop the abductions, but facilitate them by allowing Karuna cadres to transport kidnapped children through checkpoints on the way to their camps. (Human Rights Watch)

SUDAN
Child soldiers have been forcibly recruited by the government paramilitary Popular Defense Forces and by northern and southern militias supported by the Sudanese government. Recent reports indicated continued abductions of children by the Sudan People's Liberation Army (SPLA). Demobilization of children stagnated and UNICEF estimated that 7,000-8,000 children remained with the SPLA. The re-recruitment and new recruitment of child soldiers occurs frequently. (Human Rights Watch)

UGANDA
Children have been abducted in record numbers by the Lord's Resistance Army (LRA) in northern Uganda and subjected to brutal treatment as soldiers, laborers, and sexual slaves. More then 5,000 children have been abducted since the conflict started in 1988. (Human Rights Watch)

resources

UNICEF
www.unicef.org/emerg/index_childsoldiers

Children and Armed Conflict
www.un.org/children/conflict

Human Rights Watch
www.hrw.org/childsoldiers

Coalition to Stop the Use of Child Soldiers
www.child-soldiers.org

The International Rescue Committee
www.theirc.org/media/www/child-soldiers.html

Amnesty International
www.amnestyusa.org/our-priorities/children/child_soldiers

Invisible Children
www.invisiblechildren.com

War Child
www.warchild.org

Abbreviations

AUC United Self-Defense Forces of Colombia
DRC Democratic Republic of the Congo
ELN National Liberation Army of Colombia
FARC-EP Revolutionary Armed Forces of Colombia
FARDC Armed Forces of the Democratic Republic of the Congo
FMLN Farabundo Martí National Liberation Front
FNI Nationalist and Integrationist Front
KNLA Karen National Liberation Army
LRA Lord's Resistance Army
LTTE Liberation Tigers of Tamil Eelam
LURD Liberians United for Reconciliation and Democracy
SLA Sudan Liberation Army
UNDP United Nations Development Programme
UNICEF United Nations Children's Fund

Acknowledgements

Many wonderful and concerned people volunteered to help on this book. First and foremost, I want to thank Elizabeth Beresford, without whom I could not have done this project. Her hard work, insight, and support made an enormous difference.

I am indebted to Leslie Thurman at Warner Brothers, Luca Solimeo at the United Nations Office of Children and Armed Conflict, Esther Siegel for her patience and attention to detail, Betti Weimersheimer, Aimee Brill, Jane Praeger, and Peter Montello for his advice and late-night Skyping. The International Rescue Committee provided the amazing drawings from ex-combatants. With gratitude to Sister Rosemary Nyirumbe and the young women at the St. Monica Girls Tailoring Center in Gula, Uganda, who generously allowed themselves to be interviewed. Jo Becker and Mike Wessells provided helpful advice and information. Thanks also to my friends at Human Rights First, Nicola Fletcher at the ICC and Chris Lamora at Senator Richard Durbin's office, Lotti at Noor Images, and Adrian at Panos. Luis Moreno-Ocampo started me on this whole journey. Finally, thanks to my husband Nate Kravis, who has cheered me on and thoughtfully looked over all the work.

Leora Kahn

Child Soldiers

Published in the United States by powerHouse Books,
a division of powerHouse Cultural Entertainment, Inc.
37 Main Street, Brooklyn, NY 11201-1021
telephone 212 604 9074, fax 212 366 5247
e-mail: childsoldiers@powerHouseBooks.com
website: www.powerHouseBooks.com

First edition, 2008

Library of Congress Control Number: 2008931547

Hardcover ISBN 978-1-57687-455-4

Printing and binding by Midas Printing, Inc., China

Book design by Robert Avellan
Assistant editor: Elizabeth Beresford

A complete catalog of powerHouse Books and Limited Editions is available upon request; please call, write, or visit our website.

10 9 8 7 6 5 4 3 2 1

Printed and bound in China